Christian Heroes: Then & Now

RICHARD WURMBRAND

Love Your Enemies

Christian Heroes: Then & Now

Richard Wurmbrand

Love Your Enemies

JANET & GEOFF BENGE

YWAM Publishing is the publishing ministry of Youth With A Mission (YWAM), an international missionary organization of Christians from many denominations dedicated to presenting Jesus Christ to this generation. To this end, YWAM has focused its efforts in three main areas: (1) training and equipping believers for their part in fulfilling the Great Commission (Matthew 28:19), (2) personal evangelism, and (3) mercy ministry (medical and relief work).

For a free catalog of books and materials, call (425) 771-1153 or (800) 922-2143. Visit us online at www.ywampublishing.com.

Richard Wurmbrand: Love Your Enemies

Published by YWAM Publishing
a ministry of Youth With A Mission
P.O. Box 55787, Seattle, WA 98155-0787

Library of Congress Cataloging-in-Publication Data

Names: Benge, Janet, 1958– author.
Title: Richard Wurmbrand : love your enemies / Janet and Geoff Benge.
Description: Seattle WA : YWAM Publishing, 2017. | Series: Christian heroes: then & now | Includes bibliographical references. | Audience: Ages 10–14.
Identifiers: LCCN 2016058006 (print) | LCCN 2017000133 (ebook) | ISBN 9781576589878 (pbk.) | ISBN 9781576586518 (e-book)
Subjects: LCSH: Wurmbrand, Richard—Juvenile literature. | Lutheran Church—Romania—Clergy—Biography—Juvenile literature. | Persecution—Romania—History—20th century—Juvenile literature. | Political prisoners—Romania—Biography—Juvenile literature. | Communism and Christianity—Romania—History—20th century—Juvenile literature. | Romania—Church history—20th century—Juvenile literature.
Classification: LCC BX8080.W86 B46 2017 (print) | LCC BX8080.W86 (ebook) | DDC 272/.9092 [B] —dc23
LC record available at https://lccn.loc.gov/2016058006

Second printing 2022

Printed in the United States of America

Christian Heroes: Then & Now

Adoniram Judson
Albert Schweitzer
Amy Carmichael
Betty Greene
Brother Andrew
Cameron Townsend
Charles Mulli
Clarence Jones
Corrie ten Boom
Count Zinzendorf
C. S. Lewis
C. T. Studd
David Bussau
David Livingstone
Dietrich Bonhoeffer
D. L. Moody
Elisabeth Elliot
Eric Liddell
Florence Young
Francis Asbury
George Müller
Gladys Aylward
Helen Roseveare
Hudson Taylor
Ida Scudder
Isobel Kuhn
Jacob DeShazer
Jim Elliot
John Flynn
John Newton
John Wesley
John Williams
Jonathan Goforth
Klaus-Dieter John
Lillian Trasher
Loren Cunningham
Lottie Moon
Mary Slessor
Mildred Cable
Nate Saint
Norman Grubb
Paul Brand
Rachel Saint
Richard Wurmbrand
Rowland Bingham
Samuel Zwemer
Sundar Singh
Wilfred Grenfell
William Booth
William Carey

Available in paperback, e-book, and audiobook formats.Unit study curriculum guides are available for select biographies.

www.YWAMpublishing.com

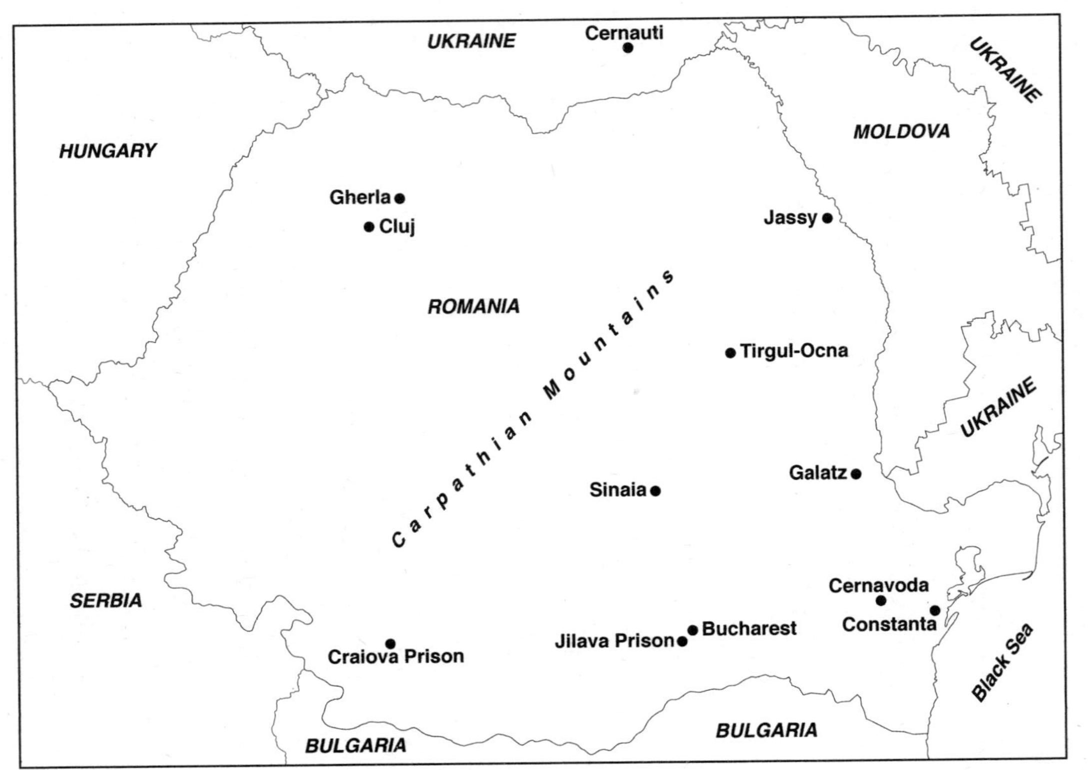
UKRAINE
Cernauti
UKRAINE
MOLDOVA
HUNGARY
Gherla
Cluj
Jassy
ROMANIA
Carpathian Mountains
Tirgul-Ocna
UKRAINE
Galatz
Sinaia
SERBIA
Cernavoda
Constanta
Bucharest
Jilava Prison
Craiova Prison
Black Sea
BULGARIA
BULGARIA

Contents

Chapter 1

He Could Never Have Imagined

Richard Wurmbrand felt the guard set him down on the cold, wet cobblestones. He could feel someone clamp a metal ring around his ankle. Then he heard the thud of a hammer against metal. It could mean only one thing—he was being fitted with a leg iron, chain, and weight.

The filthy towel wrapped around his head so he couldn't see was uncoiled, and Richard could clearly see the leg iron with a fifty-pound metal ball—about half his current weight—attached to it.

Two guards thrust their hands under Richard and lifted him and the fifty-pound weight into the back of a truck with other prisoners also in leg irons. *Where are they taking me?* Richard wondered. *Surely they can see I'm too sick to start my twenty years of hard labor.*

The truck's engine revved, the prison gate swung open, and they were off.

It was dark by the time the truck pulled to a halt. Richard and some of the other prisoners were transferred from the back of the truck into a boxcar. When the car was full, its door slammed shut. Soon a whistle blew, and the boxcar jerked as the train pulled away from the siding. Richard remembered the stories he had heard about how the Nazis rounded up Jews and sent them in trains to concentration camps and certain death. Did that same fate now await him?

As a young boy growing up in Istanbul, Richard could never have imagined that one day he would be a prisoner of the state, his body tortured and beaten. He had been an atheist in his early life, but now here he was, probably on the way to his death because of his Christian faith.

Chapter 2

Everything the World Had to Offer

A breeze blew in from the Sea of Marmara to the south of Istanbul as ten-year-old Richard stood silently watching the carpenter nail the coffin shut. His father, Henry Wurmbrand, was inside the box. He had died from the influenza epidemic that began circling the world in 1918 at the end of the Great War. As he stared at the plain coffin, Richard wondered what he should be feeling. Surely it was tragic to lose your father while so young, but Richard knew he wouldn't miss him that much. His father had been a distant man, preferring the company of his books to that of his family. In fact, Richard could not recall the last conversation he'd had with him, they were so few. Even though his three older brothers, Max, Theodore, and Lazar, and his mother, Emilia, were standing nearby, Richard felt more alone now than he ever had before.

After the coffin had been nailed shut, it was lowered into the grave, landing with a thud at the bottom. An elderly Jewish man, whom Richard's mother had paid a few pennies, chanted "El Malei Rachamim," the Hebrew prayer for the dead. Then the gravedigger began shoveling dirt over the coffin.

Richard had little idea what would happen now. As far as he could tell, his family had always been on the move, always looking for a better way to make a living. His grandparents, whom he had not known, had moved from the German-speaking northern province of Bukovina, then part of the Austro-Hungarian Empire, to Romania. His parents had moved to Bucharest, Romania's capital, where Richard was born on March 24, 1909. Richard's family still spoke German at home rather than Romanian.

When Richard was two years old, his family moved to Istanbul, capital of the Ottoman Empire. Richard's father, a dentist, was sure that he could make more money there than in Bucharest. However, the start of the Great War changed everything. The Ottomans sided with Germany and Austria-Hungary in the war, and Istanbul's economy suffered as a result.

The economic woes swept aside Richard's father's dream of becoming a wealthy dentist in the city. The family somehow managed to struggle through, and now, like millions of others, Richard's father had survived the war only to die from the terrible Spanish flu pandemic sweeping the world. Richard's mother, like so many other women around the world, was now a widow, left to eke out a living for her family by taking in laundry and sewing jobs from Istanbul's wealthy residents.

After his father's death, Richard attended school off and on, but he preferred to stay at home immersed in books from his father's library. Like his father, Richard had developed a love of books and reading. On the library shelves he always found an interesting book to read and study on his own. Among the books, Richard found a collection of volumes by Voltaire, an eighteenth-century French writer and philosopher who often wrote about religion, particularly Catholicism, and its role in society.

Religion fascinated Richard, who was Jewish. However, his family was nonpracticing and never attended synagogue. Nevertheless Richard felt drawn to a variety of Christian churches. Whenever he walked the streets of Istanbul and passed a church, he wanted to know what was going on inside and why. One day he set out to walk with a Catholic friend to deliver a message to a priest. When they reached the church, the friend assumed that Richard would wait outside while he went inside to deliver the message. Instead, Richard followed him into the church. Inside, it was dark and smelled of sweet incense. Richard's friend located the priest, and to Richard's surprise the priest placed the palm of his hand on Richard's head and said, "What can I do for you?"

Richard shrugged. He had no idea what might be appropriate to ask of such a man.

"Well, I shall get you a cup of cold water. As a Christian, I have a duty to do something for you," the priest said.

Richard was puzzled. Did all Christians feel a duty to do something for others? From then on he began slipping into Christian churches to see what was going on. He attended Catholic Mass several times, but he could not understand anything that was said, since it was all in Latin. However, he chose not to go into Greek Orthodox churches because he had heard they were anti-Jewish. He also began attending synagogue sometimes, but the service was conducted in Hebrew and the rabbi didn't seem to have time for a young boy who came alone.

Growing up in Istanbul was lonely for Richard, who wondered if there was any real purpose to life. He liked to walk through cemeteries on winter days when snow lay around the tombstones. *One day,* he would say to himself, *I will be dead like they are, and snow will cover my tomb while the living will laugh and embrace and enjoy life. I will be unable to participate in their joy. I won't even know them. I will simply not exist anymore. My body will return to the soil. After a short while, no one will remember me. So what is the use of anything?*

This question hung over Richard. By the time he was fourteen years old, he had concluded that Voltaire was right: there was no God looking after the affairs of humans. Richard declared himself to be an atheist, promising himself that when he grew up, he would experience everything the world had to offer.

In the spring of 1923, as the British, French, and Italian soldiers who had been occupying Istanbul since November 1918 began making plans to withdraw from the city, the Wurmbrand family also decided it was time to move. They packed up their belongings and headed back to Bucharest in the hope of a better life. But they did not find what they were looking for there. Richard found Bucharest to be a beautiful city with a mix of buildings in the neoclassical, interbellum, Bauhaus, and art deco architectural styles spread along broad avenues. The city also had a rich and sophisticated cultural life that earned it the nickname Little Paris. Despite the city's architectural beauty and sophisticated culture, Richard's mother had difficulty finding work in Bucharest that paid well, and so the family continued to struggle financially.

Confronted with this circumstance, Richard realized that he would have to do something different if he wanted to break out of the cycle of poverty that had overcome his family. He decided that his future lay in the field of finance, and he set out to become a stockbroker. Following the Great War, the various treaties signed to bring an end to the fighting had led to the borders of Romania being enlarged to include Bukovina, Banat, and Transylvania. As a result, the economy of the country was booming.

Richard's involvement in the world of finance went well for him, and by the time he was twenty-five, he was a well-off young bachelor. He stood six feet three inches tall and had flaxen hair and piercing blue eyes. "You are handsome," his mother would continually remind him. "Why can't you find a wife and give me grandchildren?" Emilia was eager for her son to marry and even found him a wealthy heiress to consider for a wife. This only led to arguments at home. Richard was in no hurry to marry. And when he did marry, he wanted the person he married to be pretty, smart, and an atheist like him.

One day in the summer of 1935 as he stood on the balcony at his mother's home, Richard spotted an old family friend, Elijah Osten, walking up the stairs to the front door of the house. Elijah was accompanied by someone Richard had not seen before, a petite young woman.

"Richard, come down here," he heard his mother call from the stairwell. "We have visitors."

Once downstairs Richard greeted Elijah.

"This is my niece, Sabina Osten," Elijah said. "She is visiting me from Paris, where she's studying law and chemistry at the Sorbonne."

Richard smiled, noting that the young woman was beautiful as well as intelligent. "Well," he joked, "this is a fine thing. There I was in a bad mood because my mother is pushing me to marry someone I do not care for. Now, if someone like you would have me, that would be an entirely different story!" he teased Sabina.

Sabina smiled back at him.

"Perhaps you might accompany my niece out tonight," Elijah suggested. "She's on vacation from her studies and wants to meet people her own age."

"Most certainly," Richard replied, looking into Sabina's brown eyes.

That night the two of them went to an expensive club that Richard frequented. As they sat and talked, Richard and Sabina soon discovered that they had a lot in common. Both loved music and liked to play the piano. Both were nonpracticing Jews, though Sabina had grown up in a much stricter, more observant family than Richard.

As with everyone else, the war had disrupted Sabina's life. Sabina was from the northern town of Cernauti, known as Little Vienna for its abundance of culture and art. The city had become part of Romania at the end of the Great War. Sabina had two older brothers, Maurice and Dagoder, who, like her, were born before the war. Her father had fought in the Great War and survived, returning home to Cernauti to have four more children, three girls and a boy. Twenty-five percent of Cernauti's population was Jewish. Although Sabina's family attended a very orthodox synagogue, Sabina told Richard she had outgrown her Jewish faith and considered it irrelevant to her future.

Richard told Sabina about his family and their various moves and how he was well on his way to becoming a wealthy stockbroker.

From their first night out, Richard and Sabina were inseparable. In fact, Sabina did not return to Paris to continue studying when her vacation ended. Instead, she stayed in Bucharest and took an office job so that she and Richard could continue their courtship.

On October 26, 1936, twenty-seven-year-old Richard Wurmbrand and twenty-three-year-old Sabina Osten were married at a rabbi's house. Richard's mother and his new in-laws attended the wedding ceremony. Richard would have preferred to be married at the courthouse, but Sabina's parents insisted on a religious ceremony. Since Richard and Sabina were both atheists, the rabbi did not concern himself with their religious beliefs. He simply married them.

Following their wedding, the newly married couple visited clubs and attended concerts several times a week. They were also invited to the best dinner parties in Bucharest. Richard had never been happier. He and Sabina discussed having children, but the two of them decided not to do that for a while, since children would get in the way of having fun. "What more do we need?" they asked each other.

Less than six months after their marriage, everything changed for Richard and Sabina. Richard, who had always been lean, began losing weight. At the same time, he developed a hacking cough that he could not get rid of. When he began coughing up blood, Richard was shaken. He went to the doctor and soon learned the devastating diagnosis: Richard Wurmbrand, the up-and-coming young stockbroker, had tuberculosis. The doctor warned him that his case was advanced. If Richard had any hope of seeing his thirtieth birthday, he would have to go to a hospital in the mountains for treatment and complete rest. Richard could hardly believe what he was hearing.

Chapter 3

The Last Thing He Needed Was Religion

A week after visiting the doctor, Richard was propped up in bed on a long veranda at a sanatorium overlooking the Carpathian Mountains. His job was to lie still, eat as much wholesome food as he could, and breathe in the fresh mountain air. Being still was much more difficult than Richard imagined it would be. For the first time in his life he had nothing to do. He spent a lot of time staring up at the clouds and down at the beautiful village stretched out below the sanatorium.

The scenery did nothing to brighten Richard's mood, however. Richard was angry and bitter. Why had things gone so wrong for him? And so soon after his marriage? What if this was it, the end of his life? Had he done everything he wanted to do?

The questions clouded Richard's outlook on life. Even Sabina's visits once every other week didn't lift his spirits. Even though he didn't particularly want to, Richard found himself thinking about God. It was annoying. After all, he was an atheist, someone who didn't believe in God. Yet the idea of God would not go away. Richard wondered if there was a God and, if so, was it the Jewish God, the Christian God, or some other kind of god altogether?

After a month of lying in bed thinking, Richard found himself uttering a prayer. "God, I know You do not exist. But if You do, which I'm sure You don't, it's up to You to make Yourself known to me. It is not my duty to seek You. I regret that You do not exist. I wish that somewhere in this universe there should beat a heart of love. I speak like a madman to someone who does not exist. Well, that's all." He felt foolish even saying the words. *Who prays to someone he doesn't believe in?* he asked himself.

Soon afterward, one of the nurses delivered a book to his bedside. "This is from a woman in room 312," she said. "She is too ill to leave her room to bring the book to you herself, but she thinks you will be interested in it."

Richard looked at the book the nurse had laid on the nightstand beside his bed. It had a brown leather cover with the title embossed in gold letters across it: *A Nineteenth Century Miracle: The Brothers Ratisbonne and the Congregation of Notre Dame de Sion.* He picked up the book, opened it, and began to read.

> We can never praise God too often for the wonders He works in His Saints, and it would be difficult to find any greater than those which fill the lives of the two brothers, Theodore and Alphonse Ratisbonne. Born in Strasbourg, one in 1802 and the other in 1814, into a wealthy and philanthropic Jewish family, each brother reached Christianity by a different road.

With that, Richard let the book drop onto his bed. How, he wondered, did the woman in room 312 know his inner struggle? It seemed strange, but not as strange as imagining two brothers from a wealthy Jewish family becoming Christians. What had changed their minds, and what happened to them after they converted? He picked up the book again and read half of it before lunchtime.

The story of these two brothers fascinated Richard. The brothers were Jewish, and both had found truth in the Christian way and become Catholic priests. They both shared a vision to bring other Jewish people to Christ. Father Theodore lived in Paris, France, where he preached and organized support for the mission. His brother, Father Alphonse, went to Jerusalem to work. Thirty-five years later, the order they started, The Congregation of Notre Dame de Sion, operated a convent and monastery in Jerusalem that offered poor Jewish children an education.

When Richard had finished reading the book, he began to wonder if Christians were right. Perhaps Jesus was the Messiah the Jews were waiting for.

The next day, Sunday, Sabina came to visit. "You are looking better," she said brightly as she kissed Richard on the forehead.

Richard smiled. "I hope so. Perhaps the worst is over."

"Perhaps," Sabina replied. "Tell me what you have been doing this week."

Richard took a deep breath. "I read a book about two Jewish brothers who came to know Jesus," he said.

Sabina's face turned white. "Don't say that name," she hissed. "You know better than that."

"I'm sorry," Richard said. "I didn't mean to offend you."

"Offend me?" Sabina said, her voice rising. "Offend me? You know I come from an orthodox family. We were not permitted to say that name aloud. Christians hate Jews. Those brothers are traitors." She put her head down and then added, "When I was young, I had to walk past some Christian girls to get to school each morning, and every morning they taunted me, calling me Jidanca—dirty Jewess. How any good Jew could become a Christian is beyond me. Stop thinking about it."

"But," Richard said, "we're atheists. Surely we can have a conversation about religion—any religion—without getting upset."

"No we can't. Don't ever mention it again," Sabina snapped. "All I want is for you to get better so that we can go back to our life together. You have no idea how many of our friends ask when you will be well enough to come home and attend parties again." She was silent for a moment and then softened her tone. "Richard, you have been very sick, sick and scared. You are not thinking straight at the moment. When you get better, we will eat and drink and dance again. We will only be young once. Why waste it dwelling on topics old men should be pondering?"

Richard nodded. "You are probably right, dear," he said.

When Sabina left, Richard reread the book. The idea of another Jewish person finding something of value in Christianity intrigued him. The notion of his finding something of value in Christianity terrified him. Although he was not a practicing Jew, he felt 100 percent Jewish, and he assumed he would never feel anything else. Then a voice inside his head whispered to him, "Do you really think the Messiah has come? Surely the Jewish people would know that. The Jewish nation has fostered many geniuses. Albert Einstein is a Jew. So are Niels Bohr and Sigmund Freud. There have also been so many Jewish mystics and martyrs down through the centuries. Do you really think all of those people were wrong and the Ratisbonne brothers were right?" Still, something made Richard press on with his inquiries.

A few weeks later, in early summer 1937, the doctor informed Richard that he was well enough to leave the sanatorium but not well enough to go home. "Pick any village high up in the mountains," he said, "and we will find you a cottage to rent and a local person to bring you food. It is time you started walking about, and the air up here is much healthier for you than in Bucharest."

Richard was grateful to learn that he was slowly recovering.

Twelve thousand villages dotted the Carpathian Mountains. For some reason Richard couldn't account for, he chose a small village called Noua. Once he had made his choice, the sanatorium staff arranged for him to be transported there.

At Noua the air was still, fresh, and clear, and the pace of life seemed as old as time. Men, dressed in traditional leggings and woolen vests, tended sheep on the mountain slopes. The women wore brightly colored scarfs and heavily embroidered blouses. An old carpenter named Christian Wolfkes visited Richard and brought some food for him. Christian was delighted to learn that Richard was Jewish, and he began telling him about another Jewish man whom he followed—Jesus Christ. Richard was shocked. Were there Christians everywhere waiting to talk to Jews about their faith?

Christian gave Richard a Bible. Richard read it constantly, often weeping as he did so. He had hoped to find something in the Bible that would convince him that Christianity was a hoax. Instead, he was overcome with the descriptions of Jesus and how He had been treated. Christian talked with Richard about his own faith and showed him passages that linked the Old Testament with the New Testament. Richard was particularly struck with Isaiah, chapter 53, in which the prophet wrote about the Messiah. He read, "He was despised and rejected by men, a man of sorrows and acquainted with grief; and as one from whom men hide their faces he was despised, and we esteemed him not. Surely he has borne our griefs, and carried our sorrows; yet we esteemed him stricken, smitten by God, and afflicted." Did this passage refer to Jesus, as the Ratisbonne brothers had concluded? And what did it matter, anyway?

As he tried to think calmly about faith, Richard realized that he didn't want anything to do with Christianity, even if it did turn out to be true. He could only imagine life as a Christian Jew, and what he imagined was awful. Such people would have lives of suffering and conflict. They would find themselves taking a stand against their own people and ideas and then suffering abuse and condemnation. No one in his or her right mind would choose such a path. At least, Richard was sure that *he* would not choose it. Still, he kept searching, asking Christian Wolfkes questions, and reading the New Testament. It made him feel like a child again, standing in front of the baker's shop staring at all the cakes on display but knowing his mother would never be able to buy him one. He told himself that no matter how much joy or peace there was to be found in Christianity, it was simply not for him. Richard had been born a Jew, and he was destined to live as a Jew and to die as one.

One day Christian confided in Richard. "I am an old man, and I have tried to serve God since I was converted at a revival meeting when I was young. Since that time I have desired to be a part of the conversion of a Jewish person. I have often prayed to God, 'Before I die, please let me bring a Jew to Christ, because Jesus was from the Jewish people. But I am poor, old, and sick. I cannot go around and seek a Jew.

In my village there are none. Bring a Jew to my village, and I will do my best to bring him to Christ.'"

Richard was shocked. He remembered thinking about the twelve thousand mountain villages he could have chosen to convalesce in and had no idea why he had chosen Noua. Was it possibly part of God's plan for him? He hoped not. The last thing he needed was religion.

Since Richard had so much time on his hands, his mind wandered, imagining what his life would be like if he did become a Christian. Where, for example, would he go to church? There were a lot of Greek Orthodox churches in Romania. These churches were very wealthy, so wealthy, in fact, that the Greek Orthodox church in Jassy, the largest city in eastern Romania, was crammed with golden icons, candlesticks, cups, and other treasures. The only way to keep all these golden treasures safe was to close the church to people. Richard could never join such a church. A church was supposed to be a place where people gathered before God. It wasn't supposed to be some sort of vault where treasures were stored.

Neither could Richard imagine joining the Romanian Orthodox Church, which persecuted not only Jews but also Baptists, Brethren, and Seventh-Day Adventists. In a book he was reading, Richard learned that the church's ritual when accepting a Jewish convert was to require the person to spit three times and say, "I deny, curse, and spit on Jews." Yet in his reading of the New Testament, Richard had not found anything that supported or encouraged such a practice.

To make matters worse, the Romanian Orthodox Church was closely aligned with the Iron Guard, or Green Shirts, as they were often referred to because of the green shirts members wore as part of their uniform. This anti-Semitic organization was ultranationalist, anticommunist, and anticapitalist. The Iron Guard rejected capitalism as too materialistic and wanted to establish a new society based on a communal economy and Romanian Orthodox beliefs. It considered its main enemies to be Romania's political leaders and the Jews, and it vented its vengeance and hatred on these two groups, even though the Jews vastly outnumbered the Iron Guard. Three-quarters of a million Jews lived in Romania, giving the country the third-highest Jewish population, after Poland and the Soviet Union.

While the Iron Guard was not aligned with any German organization, its founder and leader, Corneliu Codreanu, admired what Adolf Hitler and the Nazis were doing in Germany, especially in relation to the Jews. Hitler blamed Jews for the misfortunes that descended on Germany after the Great War. He considered them to be subhuman, and Nazi thugs had stopped Germans from shopping in Jewish stores. The shops were marked with the yellow Star of David or had the word *Juden* written across their windows in an attempt to bankrupt and destroy the Jews financially. Jews also had to sit on seats specifically marked for them when they traveled on buses or trains or even when they sat on park benches. At school Jewish children were ridiculed by teachers and bullied by other students.

While convalescing at the sanatorium, Richard had read a lot in the newspaper about what was happening in Germany. Every week the Nazis seemed to make life harder for Jews living in Germany. Richard wondered where it would all end.

Despite the Iron Guard's overt anti-Semitism wrapped up in the ideology of the Romanian Orthodox Church, Richard could not seem to free his mind from his fixation about God, particularly the Christian God. One day, as he lay on the sofa in his small cottage in Noua, Richard felt God telling him, "Come to Me. I will give you happiness. All your sins will be forgiven. Unspeakable joy awaits you." He realized immediately that a part of him did believe in Jesus Christ. Yet he refused to do anything about it. Out loud he replied, "You'll never have me for a disciple. I want money, travel, and pleasure. I have suffered enough. Yours is the way of the cross, and even if it is the way of truth, I will not follow it. I do not want to."

Even as he spoke these words, Richard recalled an old family story. One of his older brothers had told him that there had once been a Wurmbrand who was a rabbi. One day someone came to Rabbi Wurmbrand asking for help because a family member wanted to become a Christian. The rabbi replied, "Don't worry so much about him. Worry about my family. One day in the future, one of my descendants will become a Christian." The story was told as a joke, but now Richard didn't feel like laughing at it.

By midsummer the fresh air and good food had done their job, and in July 1937 Richard was well enough to return to Bucharest. He was grateful to have survived his bout with tuberculosis but was worried about returning to his old way of living. After spending so much time reflecting on the meaning of life, he was no longer sure what he wanted.

Back in Bucharest, Richard soon discovered what Sabina wanted. She expected everything to be exactly as it was before he got sick. She lined up party after party for them to attend. Richard went along to them and enjoyed seeing his old friends again, but he kept being drawn back to contemplating religion. He started slipping into the back of the synagogue on occasion, not sure what he hoped to find. He even visited the rabbi who had married him and Sabina, wanting to discuss with him the differences between Judaism and Christianity. The rabbi was very disturbed by this, which puzzled Richard. The man had had no problem marrying the two of them, even when they both declared themselves atheists, but now Richard was asking religious questions and the rabbi was immediately defensive.

The rabbi's answer to one question in particular opened Richard's eyes. "What do you make of the meaning of Isaiah 53, where God talks about a man of sorrows, a man who was despised and rejected by men? It says, 'But he was pierced for our transgressions; he was crushed for our iniquities; upon him was the chastisement that brought us peace, and with his wounds we are healed. All we like sheep have gone astray; we have turned—every one—to his own way; and the LORD has laid on him the iniquity of us all.'" Richard then asked, "Who is the one whom God has laid all of our sins upon? Could it have been Jesus?"

The rabbi stroked his beard for a long time before answering. "You should not have read that. It is forbidden to you. Only rabbis may read that. Please, leave that chapter alone."

"I would like to do that," Richard replied, "but I've already read it and cannot stop thinking about those words. That is why I wanted your help to explain them."

"I have nothing more to say," the rabbi countered, "except that you should not read them or think of them again."

Richard found another rabbi, and then another, to try to discover answers to his questions. He hoped they would give him a logical explanation for the verses in Isaiah 53. One man was Rabbi Rueben from Satu-Mare. They met one evening in a synagogue, and Richard put the same questions to him.

"Ah," the old rabbi said. "I see what you are thinking. If you are prepared to listen to me for half an hour, I will show you where your thinking has gone astray."

Richard invited Rabbi Rueben to his home that night. The two men sat in the living room drinking coffee.

"Shall I begin reading the New Testament aloud, and you can interrupt me when you hear something that you can explain?" Richard asked.

"Most certainly," Rabbi Rueben replied, pulling a watch from his pocket. "It is eight o'clock. We should be done by nine."

One hour went by, and then another. Before Richard realized, it was one o'clock in the morning and he had read the entire book of Matthew. And the rabbi had not interrupted him once, except to say things like "How beautiful" and "Ah, I never knew that about Jesus."

Since it was so late, the rabbi asked to stay the night. "But please, don't tell anyone at the synagogue that I spent time at your house, or that you read the story of Jesus to me."

Richard agreed, though he was disappointed. Rabbi Rueben was known for his intelligence and understanding, yet he had not stepped in to contradict what Richard read from the New Testament, not even once. Where did that leave Richard?

Even though he wanted to forget all about religion, something inside Richard made him keep searching. He learned that there was a Jewish man named Isac Feinstein who lived in Galatz, a town about 150 miles northeast of Bucharest on the Danube River. Isac had been converted to Christianity and now pastored a small church of Jewish Christians. Richard invited Isac to visit him in Bucharest and tell him the story of how he had become a Christian.

Seated on the sofa across from Richard, Isac explained that he had been a young businessman when he attended a Christian meeting run by the Plymouth Brethren and first heard the gospel. He was astonished by what he heard and immediately recognized that Jesus was the Messiah. That evening he became a Christian and went home to tell his parents. They were horrified and did everything they could to make their son denounce Jesus. When that did not work, Isac's family held a mock funeral for him, declaring that they would never see or talk to him again. As far as they were concerned, their son was dead. Isac continued working as a businessman for a while, and then he went to Poland for missionary training. After the training he returned to Romania to work with the Norwegian Israel Mission and write books and Christian pamphlets.

Richard found Isac's story fascinating and enjoyed talking to him. Isac encouraged Richard not to worry about his sin but to put his trust in Christ. "Give everything to God and you will find peace," he told Richard.

On September 14, 1937, the day before Yom Kippur, the Jewish day of repenting and fasting, Richard visited Isac's office in Galatz. He was depressed and did not know where to turn. "The demands of Christianity are too extreme. They are impossible to fulfill," he told Isac. "It's written in the Bible that he who says he is Christ's must also live as Jesus lived, but that's impossible."

Isac shook his head. "Don't allow yourself to be guided by what you see, because it is possible that you do not see very well. Only a very proud person could imagine it is possible for him to live like Jesus. As you get to know Jesus better, the more you will be able to reflect His love. That is the only hope any of us have. We should daily polish our hearts by concentrated meditation and by death. Then the beauty of Jesus will be reflected in us."

Richard knew that the time to make a decision had come. "No, no, I don't want Jesus," he said, standing and quickly leaving Isac's office. He ran into a nearby shop to hide in case Isac followed him.

Chapter 4

"I Would Like to Be Baptized"

Richard, I can see you are very troubled." It was the voice of Isac Feinstein, who had indeed followed Richard. "Come with me to a prayer meeting tonight and ask God to give you peace."

The two men talked awhile, and Richard agreed to accompany Isac to the meeting.

When he arrived at the prayer meeting, Richard felt truly at home for the first time in his life. He bowed his head to listen as those gathered for the meeting prayed, but soon he heard prayers coming from his own mouth. Richard could hardly believe what was happening. It was the eve of Yom Kippur 1937, and Richard had accepted his destiny, that of being a Jewish Christian. No one was more amazed than he at the change he felt inside as he surrendered to his destiny.

Suddenly Richard wanted to tell everyone, especially Jewish people and atheists, about his newfound faith and joy. And since he had learned to speak Russian as a boy in Istanbul, he even asked God to send him to the Soviet Union to share the gospel with Communists there, even though by doing so he would surely be imprisoned for his faith.

Richard knew that when he returned home to Bucharest that night, he would have to tell Sabina about his decision to follow Jesus. She wept when he told her. "Christians everywhere are persecuting our people. You are a traitor," she sobbed. "How can you join them? I cannot understand."

When Richard told his mother, she fainted. This was not a good start, but Richard was determined to continue in his newfound faith. He began making any excuse he could to go to Galatz and visit Isac, his wife, Lydia, and their six young children. Although the Norwegian Israel Mission operated under the cover of Lutheran Missions, it was really an interdenominational gathering. Isac belonged to the Plymouth Brethren Church, while Brother Ellison, another worker with the mission, was a former Anglican priest employed by the Church Mission to Jews. Together with a woman who came as a missionary from Norway and a group of newly converted Jews, the two men worked tirelessly to create a Christian community.

Richard was amazed by all they did. The mission ran summer camps for boys and men in Vulcan, 200 miles northwest of Bucharest. They published two Christian newsletters, one for adults and one for children, and held two services each Sunday, along with Bible studies and English classes in the evenings.

Before long Richard asked Isac if he could be baptized at the Norwegian Israel Mission. Arrangements were soon under way.

When Sabina learned of the impending baptism, she fell into a deep depression. Richard could understand her anguish. She had married an atheistic Jew, and now she was the wife of an evangelical Christian, all in less than a year and a half of marriage. Such a change would be hard for any wife to accept.

On March 25, 1938, Brother Ellison baptized Richard and two other Jewish men, both of whom were from Galatz. One was a former Communist; the other, a man who used to abuse his wife. After the baptism, Isac preached a sermon Richard knew he needed to hear. "You have received robes of white. It is your duty to keep them pure," Isac began. "You are human beings, and you will still sin like all human beings. You will not keep your robes white, but when you do sin, go immediately to Jesus so that He can cleanse you of your stains."

That night Richard stayed at Isac's home, and the next morning he took the train back to Bucharest. He was surprised to find Sabina waiting for him at the station. She even greeted him with flowers. She soon told him why.

"When you left to go to Galatz to be baptized, I was ready to kill myself," Sabina confided. "But then, during the night I became more peaceful. I can accept you as you are, but you have to accept me as I am as well."

Richard agreed, and he began praying for his wife. He also talked to her about Jesus and Christianity. He showed her that the commandments Christians were to obey were the same commandments she had learned from the Books of Moses. And he showed her that the psalms were the same psalms of David and others she had grown up hearing recited in the synagogue. Richard noted that Sabina was surprised to learn this. He went on to explain to her that Christianity was really just the Jewish faith opened up to all people. And he showed her how the Old Testament prophecies clearly foretold the coming of Christ as the Messiah. He even took Sabina and showed her the inside of a church for the first time. They also traded off on weekends. Sometimes they would go to parties together and other times to church.

On one particular night they went together to a party at a friend's apartment. When they arrived, they found most of the people already drunk and the room noisy and filled with cigarette smoke. In the corners of the apartment, all sorts of immoral things were going on. Richard was surprised when Sabina told him she wanted to go home soon after they had arrived. "We should stay and enjoy ourselves," he replied, with a slight smile at the corner of his mouth.

His plan worked. By the time they left the party at 2:00 a.m., Sabina had had enough. "Richard, take me to see your pastor right now. I would like to be baptized. I think it is the only way I will ever feel clean again."

Richard chuckled. "I think we can wait until morning, don't you? It is a train journey away!"

"I suppose so, but I'm serious, Richard. Jesus has changed the way I see things. How did we ever enjoy the company of those people and think that it was the best way to live?"

The next day, Richard prayed with Sabina, and she too committed her life to Christ. Not long afterward, Brother Ellison baptized her.

Sabina found a new peace, except for one thing: she couldn't sleep at night wondering what her parents would say. Richard took her to Cernauti to talk to them. They arrived on a Friday evening, the start of the Jewish Sabbath. The table was set for the ritual feast, the candles had been lit, and Sabina's three younger sisters and her younger brother were all seated around the table. They greeted Richard and Sabina, and all sat down together. Richard's father-in-law then stood to recite the Kiddush, the blessing of the wine. He looked very surprised when he noticed Richard, who he assumed was still an atheist, join him in singing the old prayer.

After the bread was blessed, the meal began. As they ate, Richard talked about the law of Moses, which contains 613 commandments, and how impossible it is for a person to keep them all, that everyone falls short. Slowly, as the meal progressed, Richard brought the conversation around to Jesus and how he was the Jewish Messiah and the completion of the law. Through Him, Richard explained, the truth revealed first to the Jews has been spread to all people.

Sabina's parents listened carefully as Richard spoke about the Christian faith he and Sabina had embraced. Her father engaged with Richard in the conversation, and while he didn't agree with everything said, he accepted his daughter and son-in-law's decision to become Christians. Unlike Isac's family, they would not be holding a mock funeral to declare their daughter dead to them. Richard and Sabina were relieved.

Following Sabina's baptism, the Wurmbrands began attending the Anglican Mission to the Jews in Bucharest. The mission owned an old three-story building in the city that contained a room big enough to seat four hundred people. Richard and Sabina enjoyed the fellowship that came with being part of this congregation, and Richard kept actively sharing the gospel with other Jews.

Richard's first convert was a sixteen-year-old Jewish girl named Clarutza. One day during the summer, Clarutza accompanied Richard on a trip to Sinaia, a mountain resort town about ninety miles north of Bucharest, to share the gospel and sell Christian literature. The town was built around a large Orthodox monastery. When they arrived in Sinaia, Richard went straight to visit the abbot at the monastery to seek permission to sell copies of the Gospels and other Christian literature outside the church on Sunday morning. The abbot agreed, and on Sunday morning Richard and Clarutza set up a stall outside the church.

As people flowed out of the church following the morning service, a large crowd gathered around the stall, amazed to see copies of the Gospels for sale. Many of the people were not even sure what they were, since the Orthodox Church discouraged its members from owning copies of the Bible or even the Gospels. Someone picked up a copy of the Gospel of John and asked Richard if it had been written by John the Baptist. Richard explained what it was and who had written it. People began buying copies of the Gospels, and the supply dwindled. As they busily sold their literature, Richard noticed a policeman standing at the edge of the crowd, closely studying him and Clarutza. Richard was sure that the policeman suspected them of being Jews. The policeman made his way forward and asked Richard his name. "Richard Wurmbrand," he replied.

The policeman looked surprised. "That's a German name."

Richard nodded, and the policeman saluted him and turned and walked away as Richard let out a sigh of relief. But his relief was short-lived. Soon the policeman returned and asked to see their identity cards. Richard and Clarutza handed him their cards. Richard watched as a grim look settled across the policeman's face. The identity cards clearly noted that both of them were Jews. Then at the top of his voice, the policeman shouted for all to hear, "These dirty Jews have desecrated our church and our gospel!" Immediately he arrested Richard and Clarutza, accusing them of a serious offense—selling Christian literature—and marched them off to the police station.

Since it was Sunday morning, only one other police officer was on duty at the police station. Richard and Clarutza were left in his custody and were told that the police inspector would be along in a while to interrogate them. However, the arresting officer failed to tell the other officer that the two were officially under arrest. Instead of being locked up in a cell, Richard and Clarutza were left to sit in the waiting room. When the other policeman was called away, the two of them were left sitting alone in the police station.

As they waited for the police inspector to arrive, Richard asked Clarutza, "Are you afraid?"

"No, not at all," she replied. "I'm enjoying myself. It's wonderful to have an experience like this with Jesus." Richard smiled, impressed by the depth of faith his first convert displayed.

When the police inspector strolled in, Richard stood and introduced himself without mentioning that they were the ones who had been arrested. "I have come to sell religious literature in your town and wanted to seek your permission," he told the inspector.

"Do you have a permit from the Ministry of Culture?"

"No," Richard relied.

"Then you cannot sell your literature."

"Very well," Richard said. "Then we shall take our literature and go."

"That would be a good thing to do," the inspector agreed with a nod.

With that, Richard and Clarutza walked out of the police station together. They flagged down the first taxi they saw and quickly left Sinaia behind. They had accomplished what they had set out to do, having sold almost all the Gospels and Christian literature they had brought with them. As they rode along, a smile spread across Richard's face at the irony of the situation. They were arrested for being Jews selling Christian literature, but most of what they sold were copies of the Gospels, three of which were written by Jews in the first place—Matthew, Mark, and John.

In June 1938, Sabina told Richard they were going to be parents around Christmastime. Richard was nervous when he heard the news. Before they were Christians, he and Sabina had not wanted to have children. Now, although Richard welcomed the idea of having a child and being a father, dark clouds of war were gathering over Europe and his homeland.

Early in 1937 in Romania's parliamentary election, the Iron Guard had received 15 percent of the votes, putting it in a strong position politically. However, Romania's King Carol II was opposed to the Iron Guard and their methods. He saw their political aims as a threat to his reign and to the stability of the country. On February 10, 1938, King Carol II had suspended Romania's democratic constitution, dissolved the government, and taken on the role of royal dictator. In April he had Corneliu Codreanu, founder of the Iron Guard, and several other of the organization's leaders, arrested and imprisoned. Then on November 30, 1938, news came that the arrested leaders of the Iron Guard had been executed. In the wake of the king's attempt to crush the Iron Guard, many of its members fled into exile in Germany.

On January 7, 1939, Sabina gave birth to a son, whom they named Mihai Heinrich Wurmbrand. It could not have been a worse time to bring a Jewish Christian baby into the world. Toward the end of that month, Richard and Sabina listened to a speech on the radio by Germany's chancellor, Adolf Hitler. His words were chilling.

> In the course of my life I have very often been a prophet and have usually been ridiculed for it. During the time of my struggle for power, it was in the first instance only the Jewish race that received my prophecies with laughter when I said that I would one day take over the leadership of the State, and with it that of the whole nation, and that I would then among other things settle the Jewish problem. Their laughter was uproarious, but I think that for some time now they have been laughing on the other side of their face. Today I will once more be a prophet: if the international Jewish financiers in and outside Europe should succeed in plunging the nations once more into a world war, then the result will not be the Bolshevizing of the earth, and thus the victory of Jewry, but the annihilation of the Jewish race in Europe!

Two months later, on March 24, as Richard turned thirty, the Nazis under Hitler were on the move. Just a week before, they had overrun and occupied Czechoslovakia. Two months later, the Pact of Steel was signed. This was an agreement in which Italy and

Germany agreed to a military and political alliance, creating the Axis powers binding the two countries together. Then on August 23, 1939, Nazi Germany and the Soviet Union signed a nonaggression pact, whereby the two countries agreed to take no military action against each other for the next ten years. Richard, along with most of the rest of the world, was surprised by this turn of events, since the two countries were considered political and ideological opposites.

Hitler's shrewdness in setting in place a nonaggression pact between Germany and the Soviet Union was demonstrated on September 1, 1939, when Germany invaded Poland with overwhelming military force without fear of Soviet retaliation. Two days later—in response to Hitler's invasion of Poland—Great Britain, France, New Zealand, and Australia declared war on Germany. Once more the European continent was plunged into war.

Back in Bucharest, Richard heard firsthand accounts of the German invasion of Poland from the Reverend Roger Allison, who had been working with the Church Mission for Jews in Warsaw. Roger had fled the city and made his way south to Bucharest. For twenty days the Germans laid siege to Warsaw, bombing the city mercilessly. By the time the Polish army surrendered the city on September 28, eighteen thousand civilians in Warsaw had been killed, 10 percent of the city had been destroyed, and another 40 percent was heavily damaged. Even worse, as far as Richard was concerned, was the fate of the 400,000 Jews who lived in Warsaw. After capturing the city, the Nazis had confined its Jewish population to an area of the city a little more than one square mile. Richard could only imagine how desperate the situation must be for the Jews there.

After escaping to Bucharest, Roger Allison took over running the Anglican Mission to the Jews. Since he did not speak Romanian, he relied on Richard to preach the sermons to the congregation. Richard and Sabina moved into an apartment on the second floor of the mission building. Richard threw himself into the job of preaching. He and Sabina also watched over eight-month-old Mihai and braced themselves for the turmoil that surely lay ahead for Romania and the rest of Europe.

Chapter 5

The Evil Darkness

Following the start of the war in Europe, even though Romania had pacts with Poland and France to support each other should one of the countries be threatened, King Carol II tried not to take sides. It was a delicate balancing act. The king signed an economic pact with Germany that gave the Nazis access to Romania's sought-after oil fields and at the same time allowed Polish troops to pass through Romania on their way to France to fight against the Nazis.

In Bucharest, Richard watched as these competing loyalties made Romania more unstable with each passing month. The countries that bordered Romania were all eager to regain territory they had lost following the Great War. First the Soviet Union, then

Hungary, Bulgaria, and Germany, pressured King Carol into giving parts of Romania's territory to each of them. It was too much for the people of Romania. They felt humiliated and demanded that the king step down.

In September 1940, a year after the start of the war, the king abdicated in favor of his nineteen-year-old son Michael, who did whatever the prime minister, General Ion Antonescu, told him to do. Antonescu was pro-Germany and pro-Iron Guard. He welcomed the Iron Guard's new leader, Horia Sima, as well as many guard members, back to Romania from exile in Germany, hoping that the Iron Guard's popularity would encourage Romanians to support his dictatorship. And with a pro-Germany leader now in control of the country, all political parties other than the Iron Guard were outlawed. On October 8, 1940, German troops began marching into the country. Soon half a million troops were stationed in Romania.

Antonescu and his new government, made up mostly of Iron Guard leaders, soon set to work establishing harsh laws against Jewish people and Gypsies, both considered to be inferior races. Many Jews were conflicted about what they should do. One Sunday afternoon as Richard sat in his upstairs apartment in the mission building, a young man from the youth group burst in. "Come quickly," he urged. "We are having a youth meeting, and two men are down there making a terrible disturbance. No one knows what to do."

Richard put on his shoes and raced downstairs. Inside the church he saw two young men. One of them looked Jewish and was standing on a chair yelling, "Jewish brethren! Pay attention. Let us join the Soviets. Let us make our way to Bessarabia. The Russians have taken it over. The Soviets promise us freedom and happiness. We must leave Romania. We will return with the Russian army to overturn this Fascist government."

"Stop at once!" Richard ordered. "You must stop. Such talk will get us all arrested."

The young man ignored Richard and continued. "Thousands of Jews have already left for the safety of the Soviet Union. What does it say about this man that he wants you to stay and be killed by the Fascists? He must be on the side of the Fascists! Ignore him. Let us make our way to Bessarabia."

Now Richard was angry. Many people could be arrested if this commotion continued and drew the attention of the police. "Go home!" he shouted. "Everyone go home, and do not talk to anyone along the way."

One by one, the members of the youth group filed out of the church in silence. The two visitors left as well, but Richard expected to see them again. Sure enough, they were at church again on Sunday. Midway through the sermon, they started yelling the same message, and once more Richard decided it was best to ask everyone to leave.

The next time Richard saw the two young men, they were standing at his door. "We have something on our conscience that we would like to confess to you," one of them said.

"Certainly," Richard replied. "Please come in."

The two young men settled into the couch with cups of coffee. "I'm sure you have heard that a prominent member of the Iron Guard was killed in Bucharest."

"Of course," Richard replied. He was well aware of the murder, since it had placed Jewish people under suspicion.

"Well, we are the ones who killed him."

Richard stood up. "How could you do that? Didn't you think about the fact that he had a wife and a mother?"

The two men looked shocked. "He deserved to die!" one of them replied. "He's a Fascist, and all Fascists are better off dead. Look how many Jews they have killed already."

"I can understand your coming to me if you truly want to confess your sins and ask Christ to forgive you," Richard said. "But since you don't appear to be sorry, there's nothing I can do for you. I don't know why you have come. I certainly cannot agree with your killing another human being. A Fascist is a human being and must be respected as one. If he is our enemy, Christ tells us to repay his hatred with love, not murder. You have committed a grave crime."

With that, the two young men stood and walked out the door without saying another word, leaving Richard to wonder about their true motive in coming to visit him. It was hard to trust anyone, now that the Germans were everywhere. Richard encountered Germans on the train, in the grocery store, even at the park. Many of them swaggered around looking for a fight. Richard wondered if perhaps the two young men had something to do with them.

On November 23, 1940, Romania officially aligned itself with the Axis powers. Four days later, sixty-four former dignitaries and government officials were executed by the Iron Guard in Jilava Prison while awaiting trial. Later that day, a former prime minister and a former government minister were assassinated.

The country remained on high alert. While both were anti-Semitic and extremely nationalistic, it was widely known that Prime Minister Antonescu and Horia Sima, the Iron Guard leader, did not get along. When Antonescu brought Iron Guard members into his government, hoping that partnering with them would stir up support for his regime, the orderly prime minister hadn't counted on how unruly the Green Shirts were. To Richard, the country had become a powder keg, just waiting for something to ignite the fuse.

Now that Romania was firmly aligned with the Axis powers, Roger Allison, an Englishman, left the country, leaving Richard to serve as pastor of the congregation of the Anglican Mission to the Jews in Bucharest. Meanwhile, Sweden remained a neutral country, and Swedish citizens did not need to flee Romania when the country officially aligned itself with the Axis powers. Soon after Roger's departure, the Romanian branch of the Swedish Mission to Israel, a Lutheran mission, stepped forward and took Richard's congregation under its wing. Richard gladly accepted the mission's support and covering.

He kept busy visiting members of the congregation, encouraging them in their faith, and helping in any practical way he could.

During one Sunday-morning service, Richard looked out from the pulpit to see a group of men from the Iron Guard file into the back of the church. The men wore their green shirts and held revolvers. Richard was suddenly confronted with the realization that this could be his last sermon. He decided to make it challenging. He began by talking about Jesus's hands, how they had wiped away tears, lifted up children, fed the hungry, and healed the sick. Jesus's hands had also been nailed to the cross at His crucifixion, and with them He had blessed His disciples before ascending to heaven. Then, pulling himself up to his full height and staring straight at the Green Shirts, Richard bellowed, "But you, what have you done with your hands? You are killing, beating, and torturing innocent people. Do you call yourself Christians? Clean your hands, you sinners!"

Richard could see the faces of the Green Shirts turn red with fury, their knuckles white as they clenched their guns. But they did not break up the service. They waited until Richard had given the benediction and the congregation had risen to leave. Then, as Richard stepped down from the pulpit, they rushed forward. Immediately Richard stepped behind a curtain. Slipping swiftly through a small door, he could hear the members of the Iron Guard shouting, "Where's Wurmbrand? After him!" Locking the door behind him, Richard ran down some stairs into a narrow, dimly lit basement corridor of the mission building that led to a back door opening onto a narrow side street. Quickly he blended into the crowd on the street and walked away from the church. He had managed to escape the Iron Guard this time.

The political rivalry between Prime Minister Antonescu and Iron Guard leader Horia Sima erupted on January 24, 1941, when the prime minister moved to disband the group. Civil war erupted in Romania, and at the same time, the Iron Guard unleashed its hatred and venom on the Jewish citizens of Bucharest. They rounded up Jewish men, women, and children, torturing and then killing 125 of them.

The civil war lasted only three days, with the prime minister, backed by the Romanian and German armies, the victor. In the aftermath, nine thousand members of the Iron Guard were imprisoned, most of them in the northeastern city of Jassy. Richard and his congregation, which numbered about one hundred adults, swung into action. They reached out in Christian love to the families of imprisoned members of the Iron Guard, bringing them food and clothing. Richard visited the wife of one imprisoned Green Shirt and found her on the verge of taking her own life. He was glad he had gotten there in time and was able to talk her out of it.

Each new change of government brought new rules. After the three-day civil war, the permit that enabled Richard and his congregation to continue to meet under the covering of the Swedish Mission to

Israel became worthless. Richard paid a visit to Mr. Sandu, the government's minister of ecclesiastical affairs, to request a new permit so the church could lawfully hold meetings. After formally greeting the minister, Richard made his request.

"With the Germans now in the country, I can't permit Jews to hold meetings, even if they are Christian Jews," the minister informed him.

Richard had expected that response. But before he knew it, he heard himself say, "Very well, I shall withdraw my application. Regardless, we shall continue to meet, at our own risk. Before I go, I would like to tell you something. Priests of all denominations come to see you to obtain assistance with their administrative problems. I wonder if a single one of them has spoken to you about your soul. A day will come when we shall no longer be ministers of state, clergymen, or anything else. We will all stand naked and trembling before God. And we will have to answer for our deeds. Consider then what you have to answer for because you refused to help Christians to assemble peacefully in order to worship Jesus."

Richard was stunned by the words he had just uttered. He was a Jew with no rights speaking to a government minister in a country rife with anti-Semitism. What had he been thinking? But that was it. He hadn't been thinking. He had opened his mouth to speak, and it was as if God flowed words through him. He expected Mr. Sandu to be offended and call for a guard to arrest him and take him away—another Jew never to be seen or heard of again. Instead, the minister stood and looked Richard in the eye and said, "What shall I do to be saved?"

For a moment Richard was dumbfounded by the reply. Then he breathed deeply and began to tell the minister about Jesus and how a person enters into a relationship with Him. By the time their conversation was over, Mr. Sandu and Richard had become friends. The Minister of Ecclesiastical Affairs issued Richard a permit and promised to do what he could to protect Richard and his congregation. However, given the shifting political situation in the country, he wasn't sure how successful he might be at doing that or how long the permit might remain valid. Richard thanked the minister warmly as he turned and left his office.

Sure enough, despite Mr. Sandu's support, it wasn't long before the permit to lawfully hold church meetings was revoked by the government and the congregation was forced to abandon the mission building. This meant that Richard and Sabina had to move into a new apartment. It wasn't easy to find one, since they were Jews, but at last they moved into an unheated apartment in a Greek Orthodox neighborhood on the north side of Bucharest.

Since they could no longer meet lawfully, the church went underground, holding secret meetings in people's homes and apartments, with the congregation ready to flee and meld into the night at a moment's notice. If Richard or any members of his congregation were caught attending an illegal meeting, they could be imprisoned for up to twenty years.

At the same time, Richard began writing books under the pen name Radu Valentin to teach and encourage Jewish Christians in Romania in their faith. He was able to find a government censor who would accept bribes of red wine in exchange for allowing Richard's religious books to be passed through the censorship process unchanged and then be printed and distributed.

In May 1941, Richard sat on his bed preparing notes for a sermon he planned to preach. It had been a tiring day. He had spent much of it organizing hundreds of crates of food that were to be stored overnight in his apartment. The crates took up one room from floor to ceiling. The following day Richard and Sabina would take them to the women's prison in Bucharest, where about two hundred Christian women belonging to Baptist, Pentecostal, and Seventh-Day Adventist churches were being held.

Richard was just putting the finishing touch to his sermon when Sabina entered their bedroom. She looked calm and collected. "The police have just surrounded our apartment," she announced.

Richard threw down his sermon notes, leapt from the bed, and raced to the apartment door. The last thing he wanted was for the police to storm the apartment and find the crates of food. Storing food to feed religious prisoners would surely land him in even more trouble than he already was in. Richard met the police at the door. He was immediately arrested and transported to the police station, where he learned that ten other members of his congregation had also been arrested. They were charged with holding illegal church meetings. A recently converted Greek Orthodox poultry dealer had inadvertently tipped off the police to the fact that he attended Richard's underground church services. The poultry dealer had also been arrested and was beside himself with grief over his mistake. Richard was able to console him and pray with him.

Richard and the others languished in jail for fourteen days before the Swedish ambassador to Romania intervened on their behalf. Richard knew that the ambassador was breaching diplomatic protocol, since none of those arrested were Swedish. Yet the ambassador prevailed on the Romanian authorities, and Richard and the others were set free.

Despite his latest brush with the authorities, Richard went right back to caring for the needs of the members of his congregation.

By early June, a rumor was spreading in Bucharest that Prime Minister Antonescu was about to release and arm the imprisoned Iron Guard members so that he could unleash them on the Jewish population of Jassy, a city with a rich culture and a vibrant Jewish community. Richard listened to the rumor with concern. Isac Feinstein and his family now lived in Jassy, where Isac was the pastor of a congregation of Christian Jews. The rumor continued to circulate, but no members of the Iron Guard were released. Richard hoped it had been only that, a rumor.

On June 22, 1941, the war in Europe took an unexpected turn. The Germans broke their nonaggression pact and launched a massive attack on the Soviet Union.

Three days later, Isac came to Bucharest to meet with the Christian leaders there. He stayed with Richard and Sabina, and the two men talked late into the night.

"I've heard rumors they are killing and cremating the most vulnerable people in Germany," Isac told Richard.

"I have heard that too," Richard replied. "What unspeakable acts they will have to answer to God for. I'm very afraid that Hitler and his henchmen are only just beginning. Only God knows where it will end."

Isac nodded. The two men looked at each other, and then Richard brought up the topic that had remained unspoken until now. "Please don't return to Jassy. I believe the Iron Guard will be freed, and I'm certain that death awaits you there. Please stay with us. We can send someone from the congregation to get Lydia and the children and bring them to Bucharest."

"I don't doubt what you're saying," Isac said, shaking his head with sadness, "but before anything else, I'm the shepherd of my flock. I know my duty is to stay with them and to lay down my life if necessary."

"Are you sure?" Richard asked.

"I am sure," Isac replied. "Please pray for me and my family."

The next day Isac returned to Jassy, and on June 28 news filtered back to Bucharest that the town was under heavy fire from Soviet artillery and that amidst the mayhem members of the Iron Guard, newly released and armed by the authorities, were wreaking havoc among the Jews. Not only this, but the violence of the Iron Guard was just one part of a horrific pogrom, an organized massacre of Jews approved by the government. Over the next days, Richard and Sabina listened in horror as the details of what had happened in Jassy emerged. In just a few days, more than eleven thousand Jews were killed there. Most of the adults from Isac's church, including Isac, had been taken away. Prime Minister Antonescu had ordered that Jassy and areas around it be cleared of all Jewish people.

Three months passed before Richard learned the fate of his friend and mentor in the Christian faith. Two Jewish Christian men who had been taken back to Jassy in chains as part of a work crew to clean up rubble from the Soviet bombing managed to pass on their story to Isac's wife, Lydia. The two men had been arrested during the pogrom in Jassy and forced to march in a long line of men from the police station to the awaiting cattle cars of a train. Isac was one of the arrested men in the line with them. The cattle cars had been sealed so that no fresh air could get in. The men were herded in, 140 to a cattle car that had room for only 40 men. Some men were immediately trampled to death, and once the doors were shut, others gasped for air. The two men told how Isac began to recite psalms as the cattle car got hotter in the afternoon heat and men began to suffocate. Eventually

Isac suffocated too. His last words were reported to be an exhortation to the men to seek salvation before it was too late.

After several hours the train began moving. It eventually stopped at a small station in Moldavia, where the doors to the cattle cars were opened. Somehow the two men had survived the ordeal. When they were found to still be alive, they were ordered to dig a mass grave for the other men. They told how they dug a special grave for Isac and said prayers for his family as they buried him. The two men were then taken to a German labor camp and finally returned to Jassy as part of the work crew.

Still more sad news followed. Word reached Sabina that her mother, father, three younger sisters, and younger brother were part of a large group of Jews in Cernauti arrested and transported east to the town of Golta. The town was located in Transnistria, a largely unsettled area of western Ukraine conquered by German and Romanian troops earlier in the summer. At Golta, Sabina's family had been shot and killed by soldiers. Her two older brothers were not in Cernauti at the time and survived unharmed. Neither Richard nor Sabina could comprehend the evil darkness that had fallen over their country and surrounded them at every turn.

Soon after the Wurmbrands received the awful news that Sabina's family had been killed, one of the two young men who had disrupted the youth group meeting and confessed to killing a leader in the Iron Guard appeared at Richard's door.

"May I come in?" he asked.

"Certainly," Richard replied, sensing something different about him.

"I have come to tell you that I lied the last time I visited you. I didn't kill the Green Shirts leader, nor did I think it was a good idea for your people to go to the Soviet Union."

"Why did you say those things, then?" Richard asked.

"I am a Communist," he replied, "and I was arrested by the Iron Guard while handing out pamphlets supporting Communism. Instead of killing me, they made me agree to be their agent, since I look Jewish. They assigned me a partner, and my job was to go around to synagogues and other meetings and stir up trouble telling Jews they should flee. Then, when people agreed, my partner would arrest them because they were pro-Russian. But you were not like the other Jews."

"How so?" Richard asked.

"When you told your youth to go home, they all obeyed you quietly, and we could not entrap any of them. We decided we could get to you if we confessed to the murder. But you did not react the way we anticipated. You told us we should not have killed the man." He let out a laugh. "My partner could not understand it. When we left, he shook his head and said, 'I cannot believe I have heard a Jew lecture me on why I should love a Green Shirt!'" Then the young man turned serious again. "It was then that we realized that there was no point in trying to get you or your people to confess hatred for the Green Shirts or support for the Soviets."

Richard was silent for a moment, taking in what he had just heard. The answer he had given, telling the men to do what Jesus commanded—to love your enemies—had saved him from being arrested and probably killed.

Chapter 6

Forever Changed

Richard never knew who might be at his door when someone knocked. He welcomed everyone, never knowing if the person might be seeking help from him or was there to harm him. In October 1941, not long after Sabina's parents and younger siblings were killed, a young woman Richard had never seen before arrived at the door. She was dressed in a tattered skirt and stained blouse. "May I come in?" she asked. "You are Pastor Wurmbrand?"

Richard nodded.

"My name is Maria. Perhaps you have heard of my brother, Vladimir Davidmann."

Richard again nodded. He knew of her brother. Vladimir was a young Jewish man whose father had been a rabbi. He lived in Balti and was drawn to services at the local Orthodox church, where he found answers to his many questions about God and had converted to Christianity. His father was humiliated by his son's action and threatened Vladimir, who fled to a monastery with only the clothes on his back. Later Vladimir was baptized and made his way to Bucharest to study. In 1937 he went to Cernauti to take an exam, and there he was attacked by his uncle and severely wounded by gunshot. He died several days later, but his uncle was not charged with the murder. The authorities "understood" how much the uncle and the rest of the family had been insulted when Vladimir changed religions.

Clasping Maria's hands, Richard said, "Yes, I know your brother's story. Please, sit down. Let me get you something to drink."

"Thank you," Maria replied.

Sabina joined Richard as Maria began to tell them her story. "When Vladimir was shot, I rushed to his bedside. He was in great pain, but he had a peace that I did not understand. He talked to me about Jesus with such tenderness that I felt drawn to Him. Later, after Vladimir died, I visited an Orthodox church myself and discovered the reason he died so well. He had put his faith in Jesus, and I too became a Christian."

"How wonderful," Sabina said, pouring Maria a cup of tea.

"What has happened to you since?" Richard asked.

Maria looked down. She was silent for a moment. "I was in Cernauti when the German and Romanian troops started rounding up thousands of Jews," she began. "Some were shot, but I was deported to Kamentz-Podolsk in Ukraine. We were all doing hard labor when Nazi troops suddenly arrived and began to kill people. About ten thousand Jews were there, and the soldiers said they would kill us all. It took a while, because the bodies had to be removed and mass graves dug.

"I was one of those still awaiting execution three days after the massacre started," Maria continued. "I spent the time witnessing for Christ and urging others to accept Him before it was too late. A German officer must have overheard me, because he asked, 'Are you a Christian?' I told him I was, and he said, 'Follow me. You are not going to die.' So I followed him. He smuggled me out of the camp and back to Cernauti, where no one I knew was still alive, so I came here."

"Praise God you made it," Richard said.

"You must stay with us while you get strong again," Sabina said, putting her arm around Maria. "Let me find something warm for you to put on."

Maria began to weep. "People told me you are such kind people. I believe I'm the only one in my family to survive."

As fall descended across Romania, Richard reached out to the German soldiers occupying the country. He purchased German Bibles and handed them out to whoever would take one. He preached in his underground church services that all people are sinners and need the gospel, no matter what side of the war they were on.

One night Richard got the chance to prove this to someone who had done such evil that no one would have blamed Richard or Sabina for hating the person. Their landlord told Richard that a man was staying with him whom he had known before the war. "But oh, how he has changed since then. He is like a different man!" the landlord exclaimed. "He used to be kind, but now he boasts about all the Jews he has killed. Perhaps you could come and talk to him."

Later that night, after Sabina and Mihai were both in bed asleep, Richard made his way upstairs to his landlord's apartment, where he was introduced to a heavyset man named Borila. Richard told the man he was a Christian and told him a little about the gospel. At first Borila was cautious, but he relaxed as he talked to Richard. He began to reminisce about the old days in Romania before the war and how he had become a soldier. And then he calmly said, "I've killed hundreds of Jews at Golta, you know. Lots of children and young women. They're relatively easy to kill in a way."

For a moment Richard felt the sting of Borila's words. Golta was the place in Transnistria where Sabina's family had been sent following their arrest and where they had been killed. The landlord was aware of this, and Richard noticed his face turn white as he tried to turn the conversation in another direction. Before long he had Borila talking about his passion for music.

"I love to hear the old Ukrainian songs," Borila said. "They're so beautiful, and it's so long since I've heard any of them played. It's a pity there's no piano here so we could play some."

"But there is," Richard replied. "Downstairs in our apartment we have a piano. Shall we go down there and sing around it, though we'll have to play quietly so we don't wake Sabina and Mihai."

Borila thought this was a great idea, and soon he and the landlord were following Richard to his apartment. Inside, Richard slid behind the piano and began playing the old Ukrainian songs Borila said he loved. Borila and the landlord sang along quietly as Richard played.

As he played, Richard thought about Borila's remark about killing Jews in Golta. He felt he had to say something. He stopped playing the piano and looked intently at Borila. "I have something to say to you," he said.

Borila nodded.

"If you look through that curtain into the next room you will see someone asleep. That is my wife, Sabina. You told me you killed hundreds of Jews near Golta. That is where my wife's family were taken before they were all killed. You don't know exactly who you shot, but I think we can assume you were probably one of those who killed them."

Richard watched as Borila jumped to his feet, his face flushed with rage, as if he might kill Richard. But Richard wasn't finished. "I will introduce you to my wife. If I wake her and tell her who you are and what you have done, she will not speak one word of reproach. As a faithful follower of Christ, she will embrace you as if you were her brother. She will bring you supper made with the best food we have in the house. Sabina is a sinner saved by God's grace. She will forgive you. You are a sinner too." Then, looking Borila directly in the eye, he added, "Jesus's perfect love can forgive and change you. All you need to do is turn to Him. Then everything will be forgiven."

Borila was speechless. His face, which was flushed red with anger moments ago, was now a ghostly pale color. Richard could see there was a deep struggle going on inside the man. Borila collapsed onto the couch and curled into a ball, muttering over and over, "O God, what shall I do, what shall I do?" Soon tears were running down his cheeks. All Borila's pretense, all his bravado, was crumbling in on top of him. He began begging God for forgiveness.

When Borila regained his composure, Richard noticed there was now a softness in his tear-streaked face. He shook Borila's hand warmly. Looking him in the eye, he said, "I will introduce you to my wife now."

Richard woke Sabina. He told her that there was a man in the next room he believed had murdered her family but that the man had just repented and received Christ's forgiveness. Sabina climbed out of bed, put on her robe, and walked into the living room. When she saw Borila, she reached out and embraced him. They both wept. Sabina then kissed Borila on the cheek and went to the kitchen to prepare supper for them all.

While Sabina prepared the food, Richard picked up sleeping two-year-old Mihai from his bed and placed him in the arms of the new believer. "See how quietly he sleeps?" he whispered to Borila. "You're also like a newborn child who can rest in his Father's arms. The blood that Jesus shed has cleansed you of your sins."

As they ate supper together, Richard was amazed at the change in Borila. He was a new man. "Thank you, Richard. Thank you, Sabina. I will never forget this time or the commitment I've made to God here," he said before leaving their apartment.

After Germany, Romania provided the second-highest number of troops fighting against the Soviet Union on the Eastern Front in the war. Prime Minister Antonescu and many of the Romanian people hoped that by joining with Germany against the Soviet Union, Romania would regain some of the territories recently lost by King Carol.

In mid-October 1941, news reached Bucharest that an army consisting of three-quarters of a million men from Germany and Romania were fighting their way toward Moscow, capital of the Soviet Union. Along the way they were capturing many Soviet soldiers as prisoners of war, and the soldiers were being sent by train to Romania to be imprisoned.

Meanwhile in Romania, the looting of any remaining Jewish businesses increased. The Nazis ordered Jews to vacate the houses they owned, taking nothing with them. Within hours, German officers and their families moved in and took over these homes as if they had always lived there.

Richard was glad that he and Sabina hadn't used their money to buy themselves a house and things to furnish it with. If they had, it would all have been swept away by now. Instead, they had kept a small Christian congregation afloat and paid for thousands of Christian tracts and Bibles that continued to be distributed throughout the country.

Richard was thankful for their neighbors. As in most neighborhoods in Bucharest, anti-Semitism was rife, and people weren't happy when two Jews had settled into an apartment in their midst. But Richard had painstakingly sought out their new neighbors, stopping to talk to them on the street or visiting in their apartments. Slowly he had won them over. Now they were Richard and Sabina's friends, supporting and often protecting them. Richard had even made friends with the local policeman, who also watched out for him and Sabina as best he could.

As the winter of 1941–42 descended on Europe, reports filtered back to Bucharest that the invading Axis forces had advanced to within forty miles of Moscow. Also, a rumor was circulating that Joseph Stalin, the Soviet leader, was preparing to evacuate the city. Then the weather turned foul. German tanks and armored vehicles became stuck in the mud, with soldiers abandoning them and proceeding on foot. Even then, they found themselves wading through mud up to their knees. For the first time in the battle for Moscow, the Soviets, who were used to the weather conditions, had the advantage.

Then in November snow began falling, but the Axis soldiers weren't equipped with winter clothing. Because Hitler had assumed that his forces would complete the invasion of the western Soviet Union months before winter, he also assumed that no winter gear would be necessary. By Christmas, the temperature in Russia was plunging to minus 40 degrees Fahrenheit at night. Thousands of Axis troops, unprepared for a winter campaign, began to die of exposure, frostbite, and other infirmities. Their artillery pieces iced up, and their machine guns jammed under the harsh conditions.

Despite the bitter weather, the Soviet army regrouped and mounted a counterattack, pushing the invading Axis forces back from Moscow. By the time the attack was over, at the end of January 1942, a quarter of all the Axis troops on the Eastern Front either had been killed, wounded, or taken prisoner or were seriously ill. For the first time in the war, the advance of the mighty German army had been halted.

The news of the difficulties encountered by Axis forces near Moscow began filtering back to Bucharest. Around that time Richard read in the newspaper that Japan had made a surprise attack on American forces at Pearl Harbor in Hawaii. As a result, the United States had responded by entering the war, aligning itself with the Allied powers led by Great Britain, France, and the Soviet Union. The world was becoming engulfed by war, and Jewish people in the Axis-controlled countries of Europe grew desperate. Those who had a way to leave took it, but most did not have the money or the connections to do so. Some, like Dr. King, attempted to use Christianity as a way to escape persecution.

Richard first met Dr. King when he came to the Wurmbrands' apartment with his fifteen-year-old daughter Anika. Richard had heard of Dr. King, a well-known doctor who practiced hypnotism on his patients. "I want you to baptize Anika," he told Richard.

"Why would you want that?" Richard replied.

"I'm a Protestant, but her mother is a Jew. I believe it would be much safer for her if we could prove that my daughter belongs to a Protestant religion like yours."

Richard shook his head. "But that's not how it works," he said. "I would be doing your daughter a grave disservice if I baptized her and she did not truly believe in the Lord Jesus Christ. This is not a decision you can make on behalf of a fifteen-year-old. I have a better idea." Turning to Anika he said, "Why don't you come along to our meetings and find out about Christianity for yourself? Then you can decide whether you would like to get baptized or not."

The girl agreed, but after attending a couple of church meetings, she lost interest and did not return.

In the meantime, others were sincerely seeking Jesus Christ. Horshani was a ninety-one-year-old man who had served in the synagogue all his life. Now that he was retired, he spent much of his time visiting members of the congregation he had served. On one such occasion, the young daughter of the man he was visiting gave him a copy of the New Testament. The old man treasured the gift and began to read it. Before long he recognized the Jesus he read about in the Gospels as the coming Messiah he had been praying for all his life. He called for Richard to visit him and explain more about Christianity to him.

However, by the time Richard visited, Horshani had come to understand and had passed over the line into belief and a new life in Christ. As the two men prayed together, Richard could see the joy that emanated from the old man's face.

One bitterly cold day in early February 1942, Horshani knocked on the door of the Wurmbrands' apartment. Richard was surprised to see him out in such awful weather and asked why he had come. "I've come to be baptized," Horshani declared.

Richard was surprised. He had said nothing to the old man about baptism when they met. "So tell me, why do you wish to be baptized?" he asked.

Horshani's reply was quick and sharp. "Because Jesus commands it."

"And why do you feel compelled to fulfill the commandments of Jesus?" Richard pressed.

"Because Jesus is the Son of God, and we must all obey Him," Horshani retorted.

Horshani's children were all dead, and the old man lived with his granddaughter. Richard asked him, "Have you told your granddaughter you're going to be baptized?"

"Yes," he replied.

"What did she say?"

"She said she would throw me out of the house if I did so."

"What would you do at your age if she really did throw you out?"

"I will stand out in the snow in the street with Jesus, knowing I have fulfilled His commandment," Horshani replied.

It was clear to Richard that the old man knew exactly what he was doing and was ready for baptism.

Sure enough, Horshani's granddaughter threw him out of the house after his baptism. The old man was unfazed. His faith was deep and strong. He began spending nights with old friends, enthusiastically sharing the gospel with them. Eventually his granddaughter relented and allowed him to come back and live in her house. Richard was amazed that he showed no bitterness toward her.

By the time Richard celebrated his thirty-third birthday in March 1942, Romania was completely enmeshed in the war. The country was not only sending more soldiers than any other country to fight alongside the Germans but also providing millions of barrels of oil to German factories manufacturing ammunition, weapons, tanks, ships, and airplanes for the war effort. The country also exported a lot of grain to Germany without ever receiving payment for any of it. In Romania food was scarce, and Romanians were issued ration cards. The ration cards of Jews were marked with a Star of David in the corner. This meant that Jews were not allowed to shop for food before ten o'clock in the morning, by which time nearly everything was sold out for the day. And even if there were food supplies left to purchase, Jews were entitled to buy only half the amount allowed non-Jews and had to pay twice the price for it. Jews were also given an eight o'clock evening curfew, which meant that they could not go out to earn extra money in the evening.

The curfew made it more difficult for Richard to fulfill all his pastoral duties, including visiting sick and suffering people. Although Jews were forbidden to travel, Richard made several secret trips north and east to Galatz and Jassy to encourage fellow Christians there. While in Jassy, he visited Isac Feinstein's mother to try to comfort her over the loss of her son. He soon discovered that she had lost all four of her sons in the war and was too bitter to listen to anything he had to say.

But the news that Isac's wife and six children had escaped to Switzerland was a bright spot for Richard in a country that was becoming darker with each passing month.

Chapter 7

Unknown Territory

Both Richard and Sabina were harassed or arrested by the authorities many times, yet neither of them ever remained in prison more than two weeks. As the war dragged on, more Romanians began questioning why their leaders had sided with the Germans. By 1943 the tide was beginning to turn against Germany and her Axis partners. Along with encountering stunning losses in Hitler's attempt to invade and capture Moscow, Field Marshal Erwin Rommel's Afrika Korps had been defeated by the British. As the year progressed, the Axis powers experienced more setbacks.

In July 1943, Allied forces landed in Sicily and in Italy soon afterward. Meanwhile, American and British aircraft, departing from England, began making bombing runs over Germany. The Allies also started bombing Romania from the air. On August 1, 1943, American planes bombed the Ploiesti oil refineries, about thirty-five miles north of Bucharest. These refineries provided about 30 percent of Axis oil, much of which was transported by railway through Bucharest. Richard wondered how long it would be before Allied bombers began raining down bombs on the city.

Life became more desperate for Romania's citizens, something that Richard believed to be hardly possible. He decided that the time had come to prepare four-year-old Mihai for the possibility that he and his parents would be arrested and killed. After dinner one night, he stayed at the table with his son. "You know nothing happens to us without God's permission?" he asked.

"Yes," Mihai replied.

"Sometimes God does allow bad things to happen to us. For instance, one day you and I and Mommy might all be arrested and taken away."

"Will we get to ride in a car?" Mihai asked, excitedly.

"Yes, probably," Richard said.

"I'll get to see the town properly," Mihai said, reminding his father that he was hardly ever allowed out of the apartment.

"True," Richard responded, knowing it was far too risky to let his son go out to play and explore. "But it will be a very short car ride," he added. "And at the end of it they might shoot us."

"Will we die?"

"Yes. If they shoot us, we will die," Richard replied.

"Well, then, never mind, Daddy. We will die a little, but then we shall see Jesus in heaven, and the police will not have a long enough ladder to come and fetch us."

Richard reached over and ruffled his son's hair. "You are quite right, Mihai. Remember the verse where St. Paul wrote, 'Absent from the body, present with the Lord.' If we do get shot, we will be with Jesus."

Although Mihai was only four, Richard felt confident he was as prepared as possible for what might lie ahead. All any of them could do now was trust that God was guiding them.

It was an hour before the next underground church service began. As he prayed, Richard felt he should change the topic of his already prepared sermon and speak instead about Jesus and hypnotism. This was a strange notion, one he didn't think would interest a single person listening, but he could not shake the idea that God was directing him to speak on that particular topic. He hastily began putting together some notes to preach from.

After the service, the last person Richard spoke to was a well-to-do young woman who looked shocked. "How did you know I would be here today?" she asked.

Richard didn't recognize her, and he wasn't sure what she was talking about. "Have we met before?" he asked.

The young woman smiled. "I'm Anika King. I attended your service several times over a year and a half ago. My father is Dr. King, the hypnotist."

"Yes, I do remember you now. Welcome back," Richard said.

"I found your sermon very interesting. It was as if you preached it just for me."

The next week Anika returned, accompanied by her mother, and during the service both of them became Christians and joined the church. Richard was glad he had listened to his heart and changed the sermon topic the week before.

Just before Christmas 1943, six waifs showed up at the door of Richard and Sabina's apartment. They were filthy, their clothes ragged, hair full of lice, and their bodies emaciated. They told Richard they had been released from one of the Jewish concentration camps in Transnistria and had been transported to Bucharest. Richard and Sabina immediately took the six children in. They washed them, clothed them, deloused them, and fed them. Two of the children were in need of medical care. Twelve-year-old Milo was no bigger than a seven-year-old. Richard managed to find a doctor, who gave Milo some hormone injections to help him grow. Meanwhile Betty, the oldest of the six, suffered from sinusitis and needed surgery.

One day eight-year-old Ruth, the youngest of the children, disappeared. Richard searched for her but couldn't find her. Several days later he learned that Ruth had been kidnapped by a group of Jews who were angry that he and Sabina had taken the children in and now wanted to adopt them and give them a Christian upbringing. As far as the kidnappers were concerned, that was not going to happen to Ruth. In vain Richard tried to discover who had kidnapped Ruth and where they were keeping her.

Richard and Sabina had accepted the fact that they would never see Ruth again, when once more she showed up at their door. She was dirty, her clothes were torn, and her face was streaked with tears. Tears soon filled Richard's eyes as Ruth explained how she had managed to escape her captors and find her way back to the apartment.

On April 4, 1944, Richard was once more in jail. He had been arrested along with six other members of his congregation for giving out Christian literature. At eleven o'clock that morning their trial began, but it was soon interrupted by the loud wail of an air raid siren. The judge looked up, puzzled. Richard wondered if this was just another false alarm, or if Bucharest really was under attack.

"Everyone evacuate," the judge ordered as he stood up. Richard and the six others were pulled to their feet and led out of the courtroom and through the front doors of the courthouse. They joined a stream of people heading for the National Bank Building. Walking quickly beside them were the judge, lawyers, and witnesses. The sirens kept blaring as Richard was led down a flight of stairs into the basement of the bank. Those who had been in the courtroom all gathered in one corner. The guards kept a close eye on their prisoners.

Suddenly, a loud humming sound filled the air, followed by explosions. The building shook, and dust fell from the ceiling as the lights flickered. Someone screamed. A toddler cried. Richard sensed that the crowd was on the verge of panic. "Let us all kneel, and I will say a prayer," he said loudly. Everyone, even the judge and the lawyers, obeyed.

Richard began praying. "God, we ask You to protect us. We ask You to comfort us and surround us with Your love." Then, without skipping a beat, he switched from praying to preaching. No one interrupted Richard as he outlined the way to heaven and the need for each person to be ready to meet his or her maker.

The air raid seemed to last forever, but by three in the afternoon the all-clear siren sounded. A guard pulled Richard to his feet and pointed him toward the stairs. Their moment of camaraderie was over.

As Richard walked back along the street to the courthouse, the air was thick with smoke. Richard looked to the north toward the suburb where he lived and could see an orange glow. All around him on the street, buildings had collapsed and dazed men and women stood around the rubble. Richard wanted to stop and help, but the guards made it clear that he and the other six must keep moving. They had to pick their way through broken glass and climb over tangled wires that were once the overhead power source for the streetcars. When they made it back to the courthouse, the building was unscathed from the bombing.

Back inside the courtroom, the trial continued as though nothing had happened. Each of those arrested and on trial was found guilty and sentenced to two weeks in prison. That was nothing to Richard compared to the uncertainty of not knowing what had happened to Sabina, Mihai, and the six orphans. While in prison Richard was thankful to learn that they had all survived the attack. However, about three thousand of their fellow Romanians in Bucharest had not.

When Richard was released from prison after two weeks, he got to the see the full extent of the damage inflicted on Bucharest by the Allied bombers. They appeared to have been targeting the northern train station, which lay in ruins, but many more areas of the city had been damaged as well. More Allied air raids followed. As a result, Richard and Sabina decided to send Mihai to stay in the countryside with some relatives of their Greek Orthodox neighbors. It was difficult to say goodbye as they put their five-year-old son on the back of a motorcycle, not knowing whether they would ever see him again. All they could do was pray and believe that one day they would be safely reunited.

By now Richard and Sabina were fighting to keep custody of the six orphaned children they had taken in. A Jewish organization threatened them with a lawsuit if they did not hand over the children to be raised in the Jewish tradition.

Meanwhile, as air raids continued over Bucharest, a bomb shelter was opened near their apartment.

Richard viewed it as a mission field. When the air raid sirens wailed, he would make his way to the shelter, helping others as he went. Once inside, he prayed for those who made it to the shelter, for those caught out in the open, for Romanian and German soldiers, for the Jews, and for the Allied forces bombing them. Praying for these last two was too much for some of those taking shelter, and they complained to the police. On several occasions Richard was arrested and charged with putting forward subversive propaganda because he prayed for the enemy. However, the prison sentences were always short, and when Richard was released, he would continue with his pastoral work.

Richard and Sabina received news from the countryside that Mihai was safe, although he too had been arrested. It was illegal to evacuate Jewish children from the cities into the countryside, and someone had turned Mihai in to the authorities. Richard learned that his son had spent five hours at the police station, yelling so loudly the entire time that the police officers gladly released him back into the custody of the people taking care of him. The news heartened Richard. He was glad that Mihai had the courage to protest. It had been a difficult decision to allow him to leave home, one of hundreds of decisions Richard and his congregation agonized over as the war devolved deeper into chaos around them.

One Jewish member of the church, Bertha, was married to a German man who had a Protestant mother and a Jewish father. The man and the couple's three sons were ordered to return to Germany, while Bertha, a Romanian Jew, was denied travel papers to go with them. Richard learned from Bertha that when her husband and sons arrived back in Germany, an informer turned them in to the authorities for being half Jewish. The Nazis were fastidious about how much Jewish blood people had in them. Not long afterward, Bertha received a letter stating that if she had papers proving she was Romanian but not Jewish, her family would be saved from the Auschwitz concentration camp.

One afternoon when Richard was visiting Bertha in her home, some of her relatives arrived. They were jubilant. "Look, Bertha!" her cousin said, waving a sheath of papers. "We found a forger who does great work." He put the papers down in front of her. "Send these in, and your husband and boys will be freed. They certify that you have not one drop of Jewish blood in you. You are 100 percent Aryan!"

Richard watched as Bertha picked up the papers. Her face did not mirror the joy of her cousins. Before anyone could stop her, she ripped the papers in half. "Abraham was willing to sacrifice one child for God. I shall sacrifice three children and my husband. I cannot lie and deny my heritage."

The room fell silent. Everyone stared at the shredded forged papers on the floor. With their shredding went the hope that four people would escape certain death.

As Richard walked home that afternoon, he was in turmoil. The war had created so many horrifying choices that people had to make. Had Bertha done the right thing by ripping up the forged papers? Should she have used deception to save her family? Like so many situations during those days, there was no clear answer that Richard could see. He respected that each person had to follow his or her own conscience. Everyone was in unknown territory when it came to such decisions.

It wasn't long before Richard and Sabina faced making a decision that shook them to the core. The Romanian government announced a new regulation that all orphans who had come from the concentration camps in Transnistria were to be either returned to the Soviet Union or sent to Palestine. The children were not permitted to stay in Romania. By now the six children were part of the Wurmbrand family, and Richard and Sabina agonized over what they should do. They knew they could not hand them over to the Soviets. Perhaps, instead, they should hide the children from the authorities. At last, they decided to allow them to go to Palestine, since they would have adequate food and medical care there. At the beginning of August 1944, Richard took the six children to Constanţa on the Black Sea, where three small merchant ships were preparing to set sail for Palestine under the flag of the Red Cross. The six children were among 320 Jewish refugees aboard who were corralled onto the MV *Mefküre*.

On August 6, Richard and Sabina learned that the *Mefküre* had been sunk by a Russian submarine in the Black Sea the day before. Five refugees survived the sinking. The other 315 aboard perished, among them the six children the Wurmbrands had cared for. It was a black moment for the couple. Sabina shut herself in her bedroom, while Richard carried on with a broken heart.

Richard and Sabina were still trying to get over the death of the children when on August 23, 1944, word reached Bucharest that Soviet troops had broken through Romanian defenses. King Michael swiftly organized a coup that deposed Prime Minister Ion Antonescu, and Romania embarked on negotiations with the Allies for a peace treaty. As part of the negotiations, the Allies insisted that Romania declare war on Germany. Then two weeks later, Romania was ordered to combine forces with the Soviets to defeat the Nazis. In the space of three weeks, Romania officially went from fighting against the Soviets to agreeing to be their partners and fight alongside them against the Germans.

August 31, 1944, was a hot and cloudless day as Richard and Sabina rode a tram to the edge of Bucharest with bells ringing all around them. They were on their way to welcome the first column of Soviet troops to enter Bucharest. After climbing from the tram, they made their way to where a group of people, many of them carrying red flags, had gathered beside a road. Most of those gathered saw the Soviets as liberators, freeing their country from the shackles of Germany. Richard saw it as an opportunity to reach out with the gospel to atheistic Russian soldiers. When he was converted, he had asked God to send him to the

Soviet Union to tell Communists about Jesus. Now, it seemed, God was sending them to him.

Everyone gazed down the road and wondered what to expect. Soon the rumble of vehicles could be heard. Moments later a column of tanks came into view. People began waving their red flags as the tanks drew near, until the lead tank stopped in front of them. A group of Romanian officials stepped forward and passed a loaf of bread and a handful of salt, an age-old Romanian gift for a stranger, to the commander of the tank. The commander laughed as he received the gift. A young sergeant beside him caught Sabina's eye. "Well, sweetheart, what do you have to offer?" he asked with a grin.

"I've brought you a copy of the Holy Bible in Russian," Sabina replied, handing it to him.

The surprised sergeant looked at it as Richard told him in Russian that he should cherish the Bible and read it carefully. Moments later in a belch of black smoke, the tank moved on.

Richard smiled. "We're going to need a lot more copies of the Bible in Russian," he told Sabina. He had no idea of the horrible ordeal these "liberators" would put him through in the years to come.

Once the Soviets entered Bucharest, it didn't take them long to live up to their reputation as pillagers. Soon Russian soldiers were looting liquor stores and wine shops and complaining that there wasn't enough vodka to be had in the city. Meanwhile, Richard ordered thousands of copies of the Gospels in Russian from the Bible Society and began making plans to reach out to the new mission field that had arrived in the country.

With the arrival of Soviet forces, chaos broke out in the country. Many Romanian troops and the Germans believed that King Michael's coup would be undone and Romania would once more side with Germany. At the same time, the Germans began bombing Bucharest. Thousands of Nazi soldiers and their families remained in the city, confident that things would soon return to "normal." Some Romanian army units switched sides in compliance with the new government's agreement with the Allies, while others remained loyal to the old government and continued to fight alongside the Germans. Gradually, though, it became clear that there was no going back. Romania was now one of the Allied powers fighting against the Nazis. Adolf Hitler ordered all Germans out of the country, but by then many German soldiers and officers were trapped. The hunter was now the hunted.

Chapter 8

Surrender

Although Richard hated everything the Nazis stood for, he also knew that Jesus told His disciples to love their enemies and do good to those who persecuted them. He and Sabina did everything they could to help stranded German soldiers get back to their homeland. They also encouraged members of their congregation to do the same.

Three German officers asked Richard for help, and he took them in and sheltered them in a small shed at the back of their apartment building. Each night he or Sabina took turns taking them food and collecting their toilet bucket for emptying. One night, after taking her turn, Sabina told Richard, "We must pray hard for these men. I just had a most interesting conversation with Hans."

"What did he say?" Richard asked.

"He asked me why we would risk our lives to help him, especially since we are Jews and he has killed many Jews and wishes many more would die."

"What did you tell him?"

"I told him the Nazis had killed my whole family but that the Old Testament says, 'Give love to strangers, for you, too, have been strangers in the land of Egypt.' Then I went on to tell him that Jesus commands us to love our enemies and that I hoped one day he would come to know Jesus."

"What did he say to that?" Richard asked.

"He told me that if the tables were turned and the Germans took control of Romania again, he would not show me any mercy." With a shrug she added, "We must keep praying for them."

Richard nodded. He was grateful for his wife's strong faith. How far they had come in their nearly eight years of marriage.

Within days, Richard escorted the three German officers to a rendezvous point, where they were transferred to members of the German Evangelical Church who would smuggle them back to Germany.

Not long afterward, a group of German girls who had been secretaries with the Nazi forces appealed to Richard and Sabina for help. They had to go into hiding or face being deported to Russia as prisoners of war. The Wurmbrands invited them into their small apartment and shared their food rations with them. The girls had been at the apartment several nights when the police surrounded the place. Someone had informed on Richard and Sabina for harboring Germans.

A Romanian police officer rapped on the door, and Richard answered it. "Are you sheltering German girls?" the officer asked.

"Do you know what my ethnic background is?" Richard asked.

"With a surname like Wurmbrand you're obviously from German stock. It makes sense that you would harbor Nazis."

Richard pulled his identity card from his pocket and showed it to the officer. The card had a yellow Star of David in the corner.

"You are a Jew?" the police officer asked, looking confused.

"Yes," Richard replied. "I'm a Jew, and half of our family was murdered by the Nazis. Do you think for a minute that I would shelter German girls?"

"Well, no," the policeman stammered. "Of course not. This whole thing must be a mistake. I'm sorry to bother you."

After the policeman had left, Richard walked into his bedroom where the pale-faced girls were sitting on the bed. A week later, he was able to arrange for them to be transported back to Germany.

As word got around that Richard and Sabina were helping Nazis and encouraging other Christians to do the same, they were severely criticized. Richard always responded with the same answer. "Any help given to an enemy when he is in power is wrong, because it makes us his accomplices. But we must help the enemy we have conquered."

Daily life in Romania became even harder than it had previously been. The Soviets stripped the country to help with the war effort. The entire navy, most of the merchant fleet, half of the trains and boxcars, and almost every automobile were sent to Russia. Farm produce, horses, cattle, and all the supplies of oil and gasoline were also carried off.

Through his involvement with the Swedish Mission to Israel and the Norwegian Israel Mission, which returned to Romania following the country's liberation from Germany, Richard was contacted by a new alliance of Christian churches that called themselves the World Council of Churches. The council asked Richard to be their representative in Bucharest and offered him a regular wage in return for helping the organization distribute international relief boxes of food and medicine. Richard agreed.

Unlike the Nazis, the Russians did not forbid religious services. Richard's congregation reclaimed their old mission building in Bucharest. Richard and Sabina moved back into their previous apartment on the second floor. During the week, up to thirty people a night slept on the meeting-room floor. And once more on Sundays the meeting room was filled with people for services. Richard was delighted to welcome people from many other denominations to Sunday services. Baptists, Pentecostals, and members of the Army of the Lord, as a branch of the Orthodox Church was known, all flocked to hear him preach and to have fellowship with other Christians.

In keeping with his new role as a World Council of Churches representative, Richard had a new suit made for himself. He had gone through the entire war wearing the same suit every day. The fabric of the old suit was worn to a sheen, and the elbows of the jacket had been patched numerous times.

"Do you remember the story of the rich woman and the moldy cheese?" Sabina asked him when she saw the new suit.

Richard nodded. It was a traditional story about a rich woman who, when asked for food by a beggar, gave him an old piece of moldy cheese she was about to throw away. That night, the rich woman dreamed that she had gone to heaven. When she got there, she saw a huge banquet table set with delicious food. As she started to sit down, an angel told her, "No, we have a special table just for you." The rich woman was shown to a table with a lone piece of moldy cheese on a plate. "What have I done to deserve this?" the woman asked. "In God's kingdom you get what you give," the angel replied.

"Mr. Ionescu always wears that smelly jacket. I think you should give him one of yours," Sabina suggested.

"Perhaps I could do that," Richard replied. "Which one do you think I should give him?"

"Whichever one you wish to wear in heaven," his wife replied.

Richard chuckled. The following day he presented a startled Mr. Ionescu with the brand-new suit.

Meanwhile, the war raged on all around them. In mid-October the leaders of neighboring Hungary announced that they too had signed an armistice with the Soviet Union. However, the Hungarian army ignored the armistice and instead carried on fighting desperately to keep Soviet forces out of their country. The Germans also launched an offensive and forced the country's leaders, along with the Soviets, out of Hungary. Soon afterward, word reached Richard and Sabina that the Nazis were in firm control of Hungary again and had launched a reign of terror on the Jews in Budapest, the Hungarian capital. As they prayed for their counterparts in Hungary, Sabina felt she should go there to take Christian Jews funds from the World Council of Churches, along with encouragement.

It seemed like a crazy idea, since virtually no trains were running and about five hundred miles separated Bucharest and Budapest. But after four years of surviving the war, Richard realized that this idea was no crazier than a lot of things they had done, and he agreed to let her go. The Hungarian Jewish Christians were in desperate need of help. Sabina left the following day.

With Sabina gone, Richard continued with his evangelistic work. He set his sights on preaching to Soviet soldiers in their barracks. As far as Richard could work out, there weren't many watches in the Soviet Union. Following liquor, watches were the most sought-after item among the Russian soldiers occupying Romania. The soldiers stole watches wherever they could, even stopping Romanians on the street and demanding they give them their watch. Sometimes soldiers would wear several watches at a time on their arm. And it wasn't unusual to see female Russian soldiers wearing alarm clocks draped around their necks with fine chains, as if they were the latest fashion item. Since the Soviets had managed to steal most of the watches in the country, any Romanians wanting a watch had to go to the Soviet barracks to buy one. Richard could see that this provided a great pretext for him to enter the barracks and preach to the soldiers.

Soon after Sabina's departure for Hungary, on the day of St. Paul and St. Peter, an Eastern Orthodox feast day, Richard made his way to the Soviet army barracks under the guise of wanting to buy a watch. He began looking over the various watches the Russian soldiers offered him for sale. He would pretend that some were too expensive or that others were too big or too small or that their cases were scratched and worn.

A crowd of soldiers began to form around Richard. He asked them matter-of-factly in Russian, "Are any of you named Paul or Peter?" When several men indicated they were, he added, "Do you know that today is the day when your Orthodox Church honors St. Paul and St. Peter?" After a couple of older soldiers nodded, Richard asked, "Do you know who St. Paul and St. Peter were?" From the silence and the blank looks on the soldiers' faces, he guessed that no one knew. So he began to tell them about Paul and Peter.

"You have not come to buy watches but to tell us about your faith," an older Russian soldier said, interrupting Richard as he spoke. "Sit down here among us and speak to us," the old soldier went on.

"But you must be very careful. There are informants and spies among us. We know who they are. These men around me are all good men. When someone who is not a good man comes, I will put my hand on your knee. At that moment you must talk only about watches. When I take my hand away, it is safe for you to continue telling us about your faith."

And that was what Richard did. He told the Russians about Paul and Peter and how Jesus had changed their lives and how they served Him for the rest of their lives. And when someone approached and the old soldier put his hand on Richard's knee, Richard switched to talking about watches in an instant.

The method worked so well that Richard made repeated visits to the Soviet barracks to preach the gospel to the soldiers. A number of them were converted, and thousands of copies of the Gospels in Russian were secretly distributed.

Sometimes Richard would find Russian soldiers wandering on the street and invite them back to his place for a meal and conversation. The soldiers seemed to enjoy talking with someone who could speak Russian fluently. On some occasions they talked so late into the night about Jesus and Christianity that soldiers ended up sleeping over before returning to their barracks in the morning.

Every day Richard found people to talk to about his faith. He talked to people standing in line for food, waiting for newspapers, or sitting in cafés. Richard's favorite place to talk to people was on the tram. One day he sat next to a young Russian soldier who told

Richard he was from Siberia. The two of them were soon talking about God, and the young man confessed that he had never heard anyone talk about God in his entire life.

As Richard spoke, the soldier became excited. "Ah, now I understand!" he said. "When I was a boy, I used to walk in a cemetery near our home so I could be alone. The cemetery was very old, and there was a small abandoned house among the graves."

Richard thought for a moment. The soldier was probably talking about an Orthodox chapel on the grounds.

"I noticed on the wall of this building a painting of a man nailed to a cross, and I thought, *He must have been a very bad criminal to have been punished like that.* But then I decided that that didn't make sense. If he was a bad criminal, why did he have the place of honor on the wall, in the same way that we paint Marx or Lenin on our walls?" the man said.

"What did you conclude, then?" Richard asked.

"I decided that whoever killed him at first must have thought he was a bad criminal but later found that he was not. So they had painted him on the wall to show they were sorry for what they did."

"You are halfway to the truth!" Richard exclaimed. "The man on the cross is called Jesus." Richard went on to share the gospel with the young man from Siberia. When their tram journey ended, the soldier told Richard, "I was planning to steal something tonight, but now I have changed my mind. How can I do that now that I believe in Christ?"

Richard realized that most of the younger Russian soldiers had never even heard the name of Jesus. It shocked him how completely the Communists had suppressed religion since they took power in Russia in 1917 and created the Soviet Union in 1922. The leaders of the movement, first Vladimir Lenin and then Joseph Stalin, had set about making atheism the official doctrine of the Communist Party. Many thousands of believers from all religions were killed or sent off to labor camps, and most churches and mosques were destroyed or repurposed. Schools and universities all taught atheism, and religion was labeled "unscientific" and "superstitious." Within a single generation, the Communists had turned Russia, a country with a thousand years of Christian heritage, into a place where few people knew anything about the religion.

Meanwhile, the weeks passed without any word from Sabina. Richard prayed constantly for her safety, and the church held special prayer meetings for her.

Sometimes Richard traveled farther afield to spread the gospel. On one occasion he was invited to speak at a large meeting of Christians in a village in the Carpathian Mountains. On the way there, he visited the village of Noua, where years before he had finished his recuperation from tuberculosis after a stay in the sanatorium. In Noua he learned that Christian Wolfkes had died during the war.

During the meeting of Christians, as Richard spoke about his conversion, he noticed an old man begin to weep. At the end of the meeting, Richard went over to him.

"My name is Anton Pitter," the old man said. "I have spent my life here. When I was young, I worked as a wheelwright, and it is I who presented Christ to Christian Wolfkes. All this time I have thought I had only converted one village carpenter, but now I learn that through him and then you, hundreds of Jewish people have come to know Christ. It is more than I ever imagined possible."

Richard embraced the old man, and the two men wept together.

Following Richard's return from the Carpathian Mountains, Mihai came back from living in the countryside. He had lots of stories to tell his father. Together, the two of them waited to hear word of Sabina's fate.

Then one day, much to Richard's and Mihai's delight, Sabina walked through the door. She had returned from her trip to Hungary. She told how she had ridden to and from the Hungarian border on the roof of one of the few trains still operating in the country. The train had been hauling Soviet soldiers. She told Richard of the hardships the Christian Jews in Hungary suffered at the hands of the Germans and how excited they were to receive encouragement from fellow Jewish Christians in Romania and the gift of money from the World Council of Churches. Richard noticed that as Sabina told her story, she completely left out any mention of the perils, trials, and hardships she endured along the way. All that mattered to her was that the Jewish Christians in Hungary had been blessed and encouraged.

By the end of 1944, it was obvious to all that Germany was losing the war it had started in 1939. While the Germans continued to fight on two fronts, on both fronts their military power was vastly outnumbered. Soviet forces were closing in on Germany from the east, and the British, French, Americans, and their Allies were doing the same from the west. By the end of December, Soviet forces had liberated most of Hungary from the Germans, and on December 31, 1944, Hungary's new provisional government declared war on Germany.

Richard knew that it was only a matter of time before Germany surrendered and Romania, like the other countries in Europe, could begin to recover from the strife and damage of the war and get back to normal life.

From February 4 through 11, 1945, a conference between President Franklin D. Roosevelt of the United States, Prime Minister Winston Churchill of Great Britain, and Premier Joseph Stalin of the Soviet Union was convened at Livadia Palace near Yalta on the Crimean Peninsula in the Soviet Union. The purpose of the conference was to discuss the reorganization of Europe following the surrender of Germany and the end of fighting on the continent. Richard learned of the conference from the newspaper after it had ended.

On May 9, 1945, church bells rang out all over Bucharest. The war in Europe was over. The Germans had surrendered to the Allies. That night friends gathered at the Wurmbrands' apartment, where they sang hymns and celebrated the end of over four years of persecution. The result of the conference at Yalta was that the former Axis countries of Europe were to be divided between the Soviet Union and Great Britain, France, and the United States.

Because of its position bordering the Soviet Union to the north and east, Romania was to be taken under the wing of the Soviets. Stalin promised he would allow religious freedom in the country. But even as Richard sang and celebrated Europe's freedom from the tyranny of the Nazis, he had a terrible feeling that even worse days lay ahead for him and his beloved country.

Chapter 9

Turmoil

On the morning of Tuesday, October 16, 1945, a light breeze carried a chill as Richard and Sabina walked up the steps of the Parliament building in Bucharest. Neither of them knew what to expect. Five months had passed since the end of the war in Europe, and in that time the Soviets were slowly consolidating their hold on Romania. More and more Russian troops were arriving in the country to make sure things were done in a way that Soviet leaders in Moscow approved of.

Richard and Sabina were on their way to a meeting called by the government. For the first time in Romania's history, leaders of Jews, Christians, and Muslims were about to meet together. Richard watched as rabbis, mullahs, Greek Orthodox monks, and Russian

Orthodox priests flowed into the grand meeting room at the Parliament building. The Wurmbrands found seats and waited with four thousand other religious leaders for the Congress of the Cults to begin.

Father Burducea, minister of religious confessions, president of the Democratic Union of Priests, and a member of the Communist Party, stepped to the microphone. "I declare this congress open, in the name of its patron Comrade Stalin," he said, his amplified voice echoing through the huge hall. Everyone around Richard clapped loudly, and some stood. Richard's heart dropped. Joseph Stalin was the Soviet premier and an avowed atheist. Why would he want to be involved with an interfaith conference?

When the applause died down, the prime minister of Romania, Petru Groza, stood and spoke. "I welcome you in the spirit of friendship and understanding," he began. The prime minister went on to remind everyone that he came from a strong religious tradition—both his father and his grandfather had been Orthodox priests—and that Romania's new government pledged to embrace men and women of all faiths. The government was encouraging people from all religions to work together for the good of the nation. Groza pointed out that the Romanian Orthodox Church had been persecuted during the Nazi years, but today members of the church were not only free to practice their faith but also encouraged to do so. Groza also pledged to not only pay the salaries of clergymen in the Romanian Orthodox Church but also increase the amount they received.

More applause filled the hall, and then Father Burducea returned to the podium. "This gathering is a unique act in the religious history of Europe, which, after two thousand years, has not had this kind of synod that brings together the Old Testament, the New Testament, the Koran, and the Protestant Reform. The Orthodox Church, of which I am a part, has an important role in uniting the people of the Soviet Union, Romania, and the Balkan states. This is because the government belongs to the people, the church is of the people, and all these three belong to God."

Once more the crowd cheered. And then, one after another of Romania's religious leaders walked up to the microphone to offer their allegiance to Joseph Stalin and the Soviet Union. One bishop talked about how various political movements had embraced the church throughout history, and now it was the glorious choice of the Romanian government to embrace the red strand of Communism. Together they would do great things.

As each new speaker stood to offer his praise and allegiance, Richard found himself getting angrier and angrier. How could these men not know what they were doing? Everyone knew that the Soviet government under Stalin had ruthlessly suppressed religion until virtually all the young citizens of the Soviet Union knew nothing of their country's religious heritage. Surely, these religious leaders did not believe that religion and Communism could exist side by side, or even support each other.

Richard kept waiting for someone to stand and defend his religion, whatever it was, but no one did. After each speaker, the mood in the giant meeting hall became more enthusiastic. Richard turned to Sabina to hear her whisper to him, "They are spitting in the face of Christ. Will you go and wipe the shame from his face?"

Looking down at his feisty wife sitting beside him, Richard knew she would have thought through the implications, but he knew he had to say it to her anyway. "If I speak, you will lose your husband."

"I don't need a coward for a husband," Sabina replied.

With that, Richard reached into his jacket pocket and pulled out his business card. He waved it, and a soldier at the end of the row picked it from his hand. Soon Father Burducea was holding it. "Next we would like to invite Pastor Richard Wurmbrand to speak. He is a pastor with the Lutheran Norwegian Israel Mission and a representative of the World Council of Churches. Welcome, Pastor Wurmbrand."

Richard stood and made his way to the front. On stage he stepped up to the microphone and began to speak. "When the children of God meet together, the angels are also present to be witnesses to the wisdom of God. It is the obligation of everyone present not to praise earthly powers that come and go but to glorify God our creator and His Son Jesus, who died for us on the cross."

The atmosphere of the hall suddenly changed at his words. There was total silence as people leaned forward in their seats to hear what else he had to say.

Then a commotion broke out to the left of Richard. Father Burducea leapt to his feet, shouting, "Stop. Stop. I withdraw your invitation to speak."

Richard had no intention of stopping now. He was just getting started. "God has authorized me to continue," Richard countered. "We are made in the image . . ."

"Cut that microphone!" Father Burducea shouted.

Pandemonium broke out. Voices from the audience yelled, "Keep going." "Let the pastor speak." And then they combined in a single voice and began to chant, "The pastor. The pastor. The pastor."

The chant went on for several minutes until the power to the microphone was cut and guards began clearing the hall of people. Richard was escorted from the stage. There would be no more speeches.

That night Richard and Sabina discussed the possible repercussions of what he had done. One thing was for sure: Richard had made it clear he was not interested in cooperating with the Communists. He imagined he could well be arrested the next day.

That did not happen. Instead, Richard secretly learned from a person in government that the Ministry of Cults was going to cancel his license to be a pastor. And the following Sunday, a group of thugs showed up at church, jeering through the service and yelling threats at Richard and the congregation. They were there again at the prayer meeting on Tuesday evening. One of the thugs was Isaac Levy, a young Jewish man who liked to drink, gamble, and make trouble for Christians. Richard watched as Isaac became a little quieter at each meeting he came to, intending to disrupt it. Before long he was asking questions and bowing his head as people prayed. Richard wondered if God was going to convert this young man who had come to harass them.

In Romania, everything was in turmoil. Romanian Communists represented a small but growing percentage of the population, and they were willing to use force to consolidate their power. Undeterred, Richard kept busy seeking out new opportunities to spread the gospel.

Like everyone else in Romania, Richard had noticed that the Russian Communists liked to drink alcohol, and not just a little bit but enough to make them completely drunk. From his conversations with Soviet soldiers, he had begun to see that many of them felt that their lives under Communism were shallow and superficial, that they were just cogs in a machine that left them unfulfilled.

One evening as Richard and Sabina were walking down the street in Bucharest, Richard felt that they should enter the tavern they were passing. Inside they encountered a Russian captain, his gun drawn as he demanded more alcohol. The man was already quite drunk, and the barman was afraid to serve him more drinks. People in the tavern were in a panic as the captain waved his gun around. Richard sized up the situation and approached the tavern owner, whom he knew. He asked the owner to serve the Russian captain more alcohol and promised that he and Sabina would sit with him while he drank and would keep him quiet.

The owner agreed, and soon Richard and Sabina were sitting at a table with the captain as he poured himself a glass of wine. Richard was surprised that although the captain was drunk, his mind was still sharp. As the captain drank, Richard told him he was a pastor and told him about Jesus Christ and His power to change a person's life. The captain paid close attention.

When Richard had finished talking, the captain looked at him and said, "Now that I know who you are, I will tell you who I am. I was an Orthodox priest. I was among the first to deny my faith when Stalin began his great persecution of Christians. I would go from village to village giving lectures and telling people there was no God, that as a priest I had been a deceiver, that all priests were deceivers. I was zealous in this and was made an officer in the secret police. My punishment from God is that I have killed and tortured Christians with these hands, and now I drink to forget the things I have done. But it does not work. I cannot forget."

Richard told him that despite what he had done, he could find forgiveness and purpose in Christ. When Richard and Sabina left the tavern, the captain was in a much more somber frame of mind and had much to think about.

For some reason the Ministry of Cults did not cancel Richard's license to be a pastor, and Richard kept right on holding church services. Christians from other denominations continued to flock to the services, and Richard encouraged them to love one another and talk about their faith with others before it was too late. Each night small groups of people from the church would take posters bearing Christian slogans and paste them to walls and lampposts throughout the city. Six-year-old Mihai loved to join his parents when they took their turn putting up the posters. The next morning, the Communists would tear them all down.

The church also sent small groups of people out onto the streets of Bucharest, where they sang and preached. This had never happened in Romania before, and it caught people on the street by surprise. One day Sabina and a team went to preach at a protest meeting that members of the large Malaxa manufacturing plant were staging against the Communist takeover of their plant. The following day the police opened fire on the protestors, killing many of them.

This and many other acts of violence cast a chill over the people of Romania. Richard and Sabina watched as tens of thousands of people fled the country. Many of them were Jews who had to leave behind everything they owned. Richard and Sabina's friend Anutza Moise was one of them. Through the Norwegian Israel Mission, Anutza was offered a place to live in Norway, but the Romanian government would not issue her a passport to leave. In the end she had to pay smugglers to get her across the Romanian border. It was a sad parting when she left in March 1946. Richard and Sabina did not know what fate lay ahead for any of them.

The Communist noose began to tighten around the neck of anyone with an active faith, and Richard helped many others besides Anutza to leave. Some were smuggled out of the country; others bribed their way to freedom. Some went to Palestine, others to England, the United States, and Canada. During this time, one question hung in the air: Should Richard, Sabina, and Mihai leave too? It wasn't too late for them to go, though Richard was sure he would have to act quickly to get his family out of Romania. Under the Nazis, Richard had never been imprisoned for more than about two weeks at a time, but with the Communists gaining more power daily, he knew he could be imprisoned for years or even executed for his faith. Sabina would probably be arrested too. Then who would look after their son?

One day, one of the new converts visited the Wurmbrands. As he talked about his conversion, he mentioned the verse Richard had quoted to him: "Escape for thy life. Look not behind thee." These were the words the angel had told Lot when he and his family fled from Sodom. When the man left, Richard knew it was time for him and Sabina to settle the matter of leaving once and for all. "Perhaps that was a message from God," he told his wife. "The angel told Lot to flee for his life. Things are becoming desperate here. It's a wonder I have not been arrested yet. Perhaps we are to flee for our lives."

Sabina quietly left the room. She returned moments later with her Bible. "Escape to save what life?" she asked Richard as she opened it. Then she read, "Whosoever will save his life shall lose it, and whosoever will lose his life for my sake shall find it." Then looking Richard in the eye, she asked, "If you leave now, how will you ever be able to preach from that text again?"

By the end of the week, Richard and Sabina had committed themselves to staying with their congregation no matter what lay ahead. They would leave their fate in God's hands.

Meanwhile, political chaos swirled around them. On June 1, 1946, Ion Antonescu, his son, and several high-ranking generals in Antonescu's regime during the war were executed by the government outside Jilava Prison. That same day, the current Romanian government promised the Allies that they would hold a free election and uphold democracy.

The election was held on November 19, 1946, and it was anything but democratic. A coalition called the Bloc of Democratic Parties, led by the Romanian Communist Party, received nearly 70 percent of the votes, winning a majority 347 seats to form a new government. Richard felt sure that a time of great difficulty was coming to the country. He was spurred on by the words of Jesus: "We must work the works of him who sent me while it is day; the night is coming, when no one can work."

By fall 1947, Romania was in desperate straits. The crops failed that year, and dreaded ration cards were reintroduced. The cards entitled each person to one ounce of meat per day, if anyone could find it on the shelves and had the money to buy it. People would first line up outside stores and then ask what they were lining up for. Inflation was rampant, and the government passed emergency laws confiscating all gold and emptying all foreign bank accounts held by Romanians citizens and foreign residents.

November 1947 was a pivotal month. It became clear that Romania was a puppet state of the Soviet Union, with the Soviets pulling the strings of power. The Bloc of Democratic Parties government was reorganized, with even more ties to the Soviet Union. Ana Pauker, a Jew who had become a Communist, was given a high position in the new regime. Richard had heard it rumored that she was completely heartless. At the same time, 165 Romanian diplomats were recalled from around the world.

On December 30, 1947, Gheorghe Gheorghiu-Dej, general secretary of the Romanian Communist Party, and Prime Minister Petru Groza confronted King Michael with a gun. They gave him the choice between death for himself and fifteen hundred young people currently imprisoned in the country or renouncing the throne. The king signed papers abdicating his position and quietly left for Greece.

On January 1, 1948, the Romanian People's Republic was proclaimed. The old kingdom of Romania was no more. Two and a half years had passed since peace bells tolled throughout Bucharest to declare the defeat of the Nazis and the end of the war in Europe. Now the old order so many had fought for and died trying to protect had been swept away. A new political reality confronted Richard, Sabina, and everyone else who had not fled the country.

Chapter 10

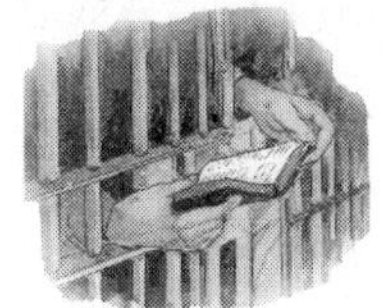

Vasile Georgescu

It was a brisk but sunny Sunday morning as Richard walked along the street before church. In the afternoon he had a wedding to officiate. He smiled to himself as he thought about the date: it was a leap day, February 29, 1948, a date that occurred only once every four years. He would be sure to mention the day in his sermon. In the Bible, the words "Don't be afraid" were repeated 366 times, once for each day of the year and even one for leap day when it came around. No matter what lay ahead, Richard wanted to remind the members of the congregation that God had everything under control, and so there was no need to be afraid.

As he walked past an office building, Richard heard a vehicle to his left pull up beside him. Two men in dark suits jumped out of a black Ford panel van. As they approached Richard, one of them said, "You're coming with us." With that the two men looped their arms under Richard's and began pulling him toward the van. Although he was much taller than either man, Richard knew it was useless to struggle. It was obvious that the two men worked for the Securitate (Secret Police), who knew where he lived. If he escaped, they would find him soon enough.

Richard felt his head being shoved down as he was pushed into the back of the van. The door slammed shut behind him, and the van sped off. Twenty minutes later, the Ford van passed through the iron gates of Calea Rohovei Prison and screeched to a halt. Richard was dragged from the van and marched into a large room.

Inside, a man ordered, "Take off your belt, tie, and shoelaces." When Richard had done so, the man informed him, "You are no longer to be known as Richard Wurmbrand. You are now Vasile Georgescu. Do not use your obsolete name again."

From the large room Richard was taken to a cell. As the cell door clanked shut behind him, he looked around. The walls were brick, and the cell contained two cots with thin straw mattress pads and a bucket. The solid cell door had a spy hole in it, covered by a metal flap on the outside. Toward the top of the cell's south wall was a window covered with a metal grate. Richard groaned. Being six feet three inches tall had its advantages and disadvantages. He was able to see out the cell window, but his feet dangled over the end of the cot.

As he peered out the high window at the sun, Richard wondered if Sabina knew that he was missing. They had contacts—Christians—in the Ministry of Justice. He was sure that once Sabina discovered he had disappeared, they would help her learn what had become of him and where he had been taken. The name change, though, bothered him. The Secret Police seemed to be going to great lengths to make Richard untraceable. How long would it be before his wife knew he was alive? And for that matter, how much longer would he be alive? After all, the Secret Police had a reputation of torturing and killing prisoners. All Richard could do was pray that Sabina soon found out what had happened to him. He didn't want to dwell on the possibility that his wife had also been arrested and that nine-year-old Mihai was now left having to fend for himself on the streets.

Richard received no food that night and was offered a scant bowl of boiled barley the following morning. Soon after he had gulped it down, he heard the bolt of the cell door being drawn. The door swung open, and there stood a tall man with jet black hair and a distinctive widow's peak. Richard recognized him immediately. It was Lucretiu Patrascanu, Romania's minister of justice. Richard was surprised. What had he done that his first interrogation was going to be carried out by a top government official?

Instead of calling Richard out of the cell to go for interrogation, Patrascanu stepped into the cell as the door slammed shut behind him. He nodded at Richard and sat on the other cot. It was then that Richard realized that the minister of justice's belt, tie, and shoelaces were missing. Patrascanu was not there to interrogate him; they were fellow prisoners.

It took Richard a few moments to comprehend that he was indeed sharing a prison cell with the current minister of justice, a man who had done perhaps more than anyone else to bring Communism to Romania. "What are you doing here?" Richard asked.

Patrascanu spoke in a clear, clipped voice. "It's not my first time in a prison. This time it was Teohari Georgescu, minister of the interior, who denounced me as a potential traitor. The minister of finance and Ana Pauker took his side. It's been their plan for some time, I think. This morning a new driver was waiting in my car. He told me my regular chauffeur was ill. I got into the car, and two members of the Securitate got in after me. And now I am here." He shrugged his shoulders. "The wheel will take another turn, and I will be out soon," he added, setting his steely blue eyes on Richard.

Two hours later the food wagon again came rattling down the corridor, stopping in front of the cell. Soon the door opened, and Richard was handed a bowl of boiled millet. Meanwhile, Patrascanu received a plate laden with carved chicken, cheese, and fruit, along with a bottle of red wine and a glass. He took the platter and wine and laughed as he set the food on his cot. "You can eat the food," he told Richard. "I have no appetite. I'll drink the wine instead."

Richard savored every bite of the food. In or out of prison, he couldn't remember the last time he had tasted foreign cheese or an orange.

As Richard ate, Patrascanu told jokes about the Communist Party, to which he belonged. "Did you hear the one about the Swiss senator who wanted to be minister of the navy?"

"No," Richard replied.

"He told his prime minister, but the prime minister said, 'You cannot be minister of the navy. Switzerland is landlocked. It has no navy.' 'Well,' the Swiss senator said, 'if Romania can have a minister of justice, I don't see why we shouldn't have a minister of the navy.'" Patrascanu roared with laughter.

After listening to the joke, Richard wondered what guilt the man must bear to lead him to make jokes about himself.

The following morning a guard came for the minister of justice. Richard waited all day to see if he would be returned to the cell. Late in the evening, Patrascanu was shown back to the cell, and he was in a bad mood. "They took me back to the university. I am sure you know I'm a lawyer and I teach several classes there. They made me teach today. I had to pretend nothing was wrong. They did give me back my belt, tie, and shoelaces but took them off me again upon my return."

Richard looked down at the man's muddy shoes. Sure enough, no laces.

That night the two men talked more. Richard found his cellmate likable as a person, though he was aware that Patrascanu had ordered the killing of thousands of political opponents. Richard was surprised to learn why the minister of justice had ended up in prison.

"We must have standards," Patrascanu told Richard. "The other day I heard a rumor that we were torturing prisoners, and I asked an official from the Ministry of the Interior if that was correct. 'Of course!' the official said. 'If they are against the great revolution, they deserve no pity, especially if they are holding back valuable information. We will do whatever is necessary to get them to speak up.' I was deeply disturbed by this and asked the official if the minister of the interior thought this right, because I did not. Had we struggled all these years to liberate men, only to torture those who disagreed with us? Does that make us any better than those who came before?"

"Those are good questions," Richard said.

"Apparently not," Patrascanu replied dryly. "Our conversation was reported back to Teohari Georgescu, and here I am."

"That is the problem," Richard countered. "At its beginning, Communism is all about the idea of freeing poor people from the bondage of the upper classes. But then once Communists are in power, they forget all about freedom and oppress anyone who does not agree with them. They have to keep themselves in power using lies, threats, and torture. Look at me. What have I done wrong? Nothing except preach the gospel of peace. You know, I'm sure, that Karl Marx said 'Religion is the opium of the people.'"

"Yes, of course," Patrascanu replied. "It is perhaps his most famous quote."

"Did you also know that in the sentence immediately before that he says, 'Religion is the sigh of the oppressed creature, the heart of a heartless world, just as it is the spirit of a spiritless situation'?"

"No, that is interesting," Patrascanu commented.

The two men continued to talk well into the night. Sometimes the minister of justice argued fiercely against all religions, and at other times he sat quietly and listened to what Richard had to say.

The following day it was Richard's turn to leave the cell. "Vasile Georgescu," a guard yelled after entering the cell and staring at his clipboard. "Put these on," he said, holding out a pair of blackout goggles to Richard, who put them on. It was impossible for him to see anything through them as the guard shoved him forward out of the cell. "Head to the right," he commanded.

After stumbling along a corridor and making several turns, Richard heard a door creak shut behind him. "Sit down. Then take off your goggles," a voice barked.

Richard sat down hard on the chair. A bright overhead light made his eyes water as he removed the goggles. Then a pen and several sheets of paper were thrust in front of him. "I have been waiting for you, Vasile Georgescu. You are a priest. You know all about confession. Now it is your turn to confess. Write down on this paper everything you need to tell us."

Richard picked up the pen and began to write. The words came easily. He wrote about his childhood and how he had decided to make as much money as possible when he grew up. He wrote about how he got sick with tuberculosis and started to think seriously about the meaning of life and the claims of Jesus Christ. As Richard wrote, he prayed that whoever read his words would think about the same questions.

After an hour an interrogator stepped forward and took away the pen. "That's enough for now," he said. "Take him back to his cell."

Richard put the blackout goggles back on, and the guard led him back to the cell.

Neither Richard nor Patrascanu was taken from the cell over the next few days, leaving the two men plenty of time to discuss their different views on life. Richard was not surprised that Patrascanu, a notoriously private man, wanted to talk about his family. Richard already knew that his wife, Elena, was a Jew who had joined the Orthodox Church at the beginning of World War II to escape persecution. What he didn't know was that as a student at school, Patrascanu had tried to live the Christian life but in the end found it too difficult. "Your Jesus asks too much," he told Richard. He went on to explain that he had never been a popular boy and that the ridicule he felt from fellow students had left him feeling bitter about life. He had eventually joined and then became an active member of the Communist Party because party members welcomed and accepted him.

"Then you are like Marx and Lenin," Richard told him. "Their ideas and actions stemmed from the way they were treated early in life. They took their bitterness and used it to tear down and destroy what they perceived made them feel that way. But there are those who have taken their bitterness and defeat and turned to Christ, drawn to Him by love and forgiveness and not by bitterness and hatred. That is the difference between you and me."

The following day guards came and took Lucretiu Patrascanu away. He did not return to the cell.

Meanwhile, Richard was taken to have his head shaved. As he sat in the chair, the barber bent over and whispered in his ear, "Sabina sends you greetings. She is free and well." Richard's heart soared. His greatest fear had been that Sabina was suffering in prison as well.

Back in his cell that night, Richard thanked God for the barber and his bravery in passing along the information.

Within days, the kind of interrogation Richard had expected began. He was taken from his cell and questioned closely by various interrogators. When Richard asked what he was accused of, one of the interrogators slapped his hand on the table and said, "You know what you've done. Now confess. Get it off your chest." But Richard had nothing to say, and he was returned to his cell.

The interrogations continued, and at each session Richard was bombarded with question after question, which he often tried to deflect with a question for the interrogator. One month passed, then another, until Richard wore down the patience of the Securitate and was taken to see Colonel Misu Dulgheru, the Securitate's chief interrogator. The colonel sat at a large wooden desk across from Richard and calmly began asking him questions about a Red Army soldier who had been caught smuggling Bibles into Russia. Richard knew the soldier, who had been converted and whom Richard had secretly baptized. But it was clear from the questions he was being asked that the soldier had not given the Securitate the information they sought. Richard was careful not to give them any information about the smuggling either. He could see that the lack of information frustrated Colonel Dulgheru, who wanted to know how Bibles were being smuggled from Romania to Russia.

When Richard returned to his cell, the cots had been removed, and he was forced to spend the night sitting on a hard wooden chair. Throughout the night, guards pulled open the metal cover on the spy hole in the cell door. If they found Richard dozing, they would enter the cell and shake him awake. That night Richard had an hour's sleep at most, and on the nights that followed he got even less. Richard was so tired he could barely think straight. Often during the day he was forced to stand facing the cell wall with his arms above his head. His legs began to swell, and his shoulders throbbed with pain. And when he collapsed from fatigue, a guard would rush in and kick him and force him to stand again.

Still, when he was taken for interrogation, Richard would not give the Securitate the information they sought. So they ramped up their torture and forced Richard to walk round and round the perimeter of his cell for hour after hour. His feet throbbed with every step he took, and when he could walk no more, they forced him to crawl on his hands and knees.

One agonizing day followed another. For comfort and courage, Richard tried his best to concentrate his tired and now foggy mind on Jesus and Bible stories. His body ached, he was weak from being given little to eat, and he had hardly slept in almost a month, but he knew he must not give in.

The interrogators were unrelenting. They placed a hood over Richard's head and ordered him to squat. Then they tied him up in that position and put a pole through the crooks of his elbows. They then hung him on a frame so that his head was down and the soles of his feet up. After that, someone began beating the soles of his feet with a cane. Richard passed out from the excruciating pain. When he later came to on the floor of his cell, his feet throbbed and his soles were bruised and cut from the beatings. The pain was too great to walk. All he could do was lie on the floor.

There was more to come. Two days later he was taken from his cell to a room where Major Brinzaru, Colonel Dulgheru's assistant, gave him a beating with a nylon whip. Once more Richard passed out as he was being tortured.

His body beaten and broken, his mind on the edge of collapse, Richard decided to give his interrogators what they sought—names. He wrote down a list of names on a sheet of paper and handed it over, much to Colonel Dulgheru's delight.

Richard passed several days without any more torture, allowing him to recover some of his strength.

But he knew it wouldn't last. Sure enough, after the Securitate had investigated the names on the list, Richard was taken from his cell and beaten again with the whip. The names he had written on the list were those of men and women who he knew had fled Romania to the West or were dead.

After being returned to his cell, Richard sat on the floor and wept. He wasn't sure how much more torture his mind and body could endure.

Later that night Colonel Dulgheru came to his cell. He looked down at Richard and said to him, "Why don't you just give in?" a tinge of pity in his voice. "It's pointless. You are only human, and you will break in the end."

Chapter 11

On the Tree of Silence

In early October 1948, Richard was led from his cell out into the prison yard, where about thirty other prisoners were already gathered. It was a cold, gray day, and the men all stood around in the falling sleet. Some had on winter coats, but most, like Richard, were clad in thin, tattered clothes. Richard gazed around at the faces of the other men, hoping to see someone he recognized. It was hard to tell, however, since they all looked the same—tired and gaunt. Still, he was glad to be standing with the others. It was the first time he had stood among a group of other men in the seven months since he had been imprisoned.

"No talking," Richard heard a guard yell. Slowly he eased his way into the center of the group of prisoners. *Perhaps,* he thought, *someone might be able to whisper there.* But no one risked it.

"Forward, march," another guard barked, and Richard shuffled toward the gate with the rest of the men. They were leaving the prison. But for where?

Outside the gate the men were loaded into the back of a truck covered by a green canvas top and sides, with two wooden benches running the length of the truck bed on either side. The prisoners took their place on the benches, with a guard carrying a rifle perched at the end of each bench. As they drove off, the noise of the truck's engine muffled the sound of the prisoners as they swapped snippets of information without the guards noticing. Richard's heart soared when he learned that the British had left Palestine and an independent State of Israel had been declared. For the first time in over nineteen hundred years, the Jews had a homeland of their own.

The truck ride was short. The men were herded down from the back of the truck at gunpoint and were soon standing in a courtyard in front of Uranus Prison, the Securitate jail in the center of Bucharest. The prisoners were led into the prison through a side door and then down two long, steep flights of stairs. Richard had no idea that the place had such a deep, dungeonlike basement.

"This is yours, Vasile Georgescu," a guard said, pushing Richard into a small, dimly lit room. Inside, Richard sat down on a lumpy straw pallet and looked around. He was alone in a small concrete room. Above the bed hung a single electric light bulb, and the end of a pipe protruded high on the wall. Richard put his hand over the pipe and felt cold air coming in through it. There was no bucket in the cell to use as a toilet. That was a problem. Richard knew from experience that the guards didn't always come when you signaled for them to take you to the toilet. He looked around the room again and sighed. No doubt he would have to use a corner in an emergency.

As time went by, Richard sat and thought about the new State of Israel. He wondered how many of his friends and relatives might make it there. Perhaps Sabina and Mihai would be able to escape to freedom and safety in Israel. Richard wondered if he would ever again enjoy freedom.

After a day in his new cell, Richard realized that everything around him was silent. Through the grill on his cell door he could see the shadow of a guard walking back and forth, but the guard made no sound, not even the scuffing of his boots on the floor as he paced. There was no noise from jingling keys or rain falling against a window, no yelling from the courtyard or birds squawking overhead. Richard could hear only the sound of his heart beating. He was in a dungeon cell thirty feet below ground, and without sound, it felt to him as though he had been buried alive.

When a guard at last opened the cell door to bring him a few morsels of food, Richard noticed that he had felt pads on the soles of his boots to muffle the sound of walking. The only deliberate sound Richard heard in his cell was the prison bell ringing to signal morning and night.

In his new cell, Richard decided to stay up at night, and he developed a routine to follow. After the night bell sounded, he began praying, thanking God for his life and the opportunities He brought into it. Then he preached a sermon—a new one every night. As he spoke, he imagined a "great cloud of witnesses"—Christian martyrs from times gone by—all listening to him.

Following the sermon, Richard asked God to send to Sabina the words he had just spoken and his love for her. Then he spoke to Sabina and Mihai as if they were sitting beside him. He knew at the very least the authorities would be pressuring Sabina to divorce him, that is, if the Communists hadn't already told her he was dead. Next, Richard danced. He remembered how King David had danced before the Lord, and he decided to do the same. On the first night that he did this, the guard was so shocked he brought Richard a large chunk of bread and cheese. Richard savored every mouthful. What a treat it was after the black bread and watery cabbage soup he was usually served.

Once he had exhausted himself dancing, Richard spent an hour or more thinking about the people arrayed against him. He imagined being one of his interrogators or the guard outside his cell. He thought of many excuses as to why they were in such a horrible line of work. Perhaps they had no choice. Perhaps their family would starve if they didn't do it. Maybe they had been tricked into the job, and it was now too late to get out of it. After an hour or more of trying to see things from their perspective, Richard came away with a renewed love for the guards and interrogators and a desire to share the gospel with them in a way they could understand.

Sometimes in the early hours of the morning, to keep his mind active, Richard would switch from spiritual activities to chess. He molded two sets of chess pieces from the black bread he was served, coloring one set white by rubbing them along the chalky concrete wall of his cell. Then he would play game after game of chess, disciplining himself to "forget" the moves his "opponent" had just made.

By the time the morning bell rang, Richard was tired. Since the days seemed much longer to him than the nights, he gladly lay down to sleep away a good part of the day. Since all he had to go by was the bell, he could never really tell whether it was light or dark outside.

After several weeks, Richard came to accept the silence and solitude of his cell. He remembered the Arab saying "On the tree of silence hangs the fruit of peace" and verse 10 of Psalm 46: "Be still, and know that I am God." Although he was cold and nearly starving, he was determined to make the most of this time alone with God.

One night, after he had finished his sermon, Richard heard a *tap, tap* on the wall. He listened carefully. Was it someone deliberately making a noise? The tapping stopped. Richard tapped back. The tapping began again. Someone was there!

Richard worked out that the prisoner on the other side of the cell wall was using a simple code that assigned letters of the alphabet different numbers of taps. It was a long and tedious way to send or receive a message, but Richard didn't care—he was actually communicating with another human being.

After several nights of tapping messages, the other prisoner, who said he was a radio engineer awaiting trial, taught Richard Morse code. It was slow at first as Richard memorized the code, but soon they were able to communicate much more rapidly. Richard comforted the engineer by tapping him Bible verses, and the engineer asked if he could confess his sins to Richard. The men also used Morse code to tap out moves in a chess game and to exchange jokes.

One night the engineer did not tap on the wall. After a couple of nights of silence, Richard tapped again, and someone else answered. Since this person did not know Morse code, Richard used the simpler code to communicate with him and teach him Morse code.

It was wonderful having another person to communicate with. One day the prisoner in the next cell tapped out that it was April 10, 1949, Palm Sunday, the beginning of Holy Week. Richard was thankful to know that Easter was approaching. He meditated and preached to himself on the suffering of Christ. On Good Friday morning he found a nail on the floor in the bathroom. Taking it back to his cell, Richard scratched "Jesus" on the wall to remind himself that Christ had risen. He also hoped it would encourage the next prisoner who occupied the cell.

When the guard saw what Richard had done, he was furious. "How dare you do such a thing!" he yelled. "You are going to the *carcer*."

Richard was taken from his cell and marched down the corridor to a cupboard in the wall—the carcer. It was about twenty inches square inside and tall enough for a man to stand up in. Richard was put into the cupboard, and the door closed. Inside, it was pitch-black, except for several narrow shafts of light that penetrated the darkness through air holes drilled in the door. As Richard tried to adjust his position inside the carcer, he felt something stab his back. He lurched forward and was stabbed again, this time in the chest.

After regaining his balance, Richard felt the surfaces around him. Sharp metal spikes were sticking out of all the upright surfaces of the cupboard. The only way to avoid being stabbed by the spikes was to stand tall and rigid. Richard tried to do this, but standing up straight was painful. His feet throbbed, and all his torture-ravaged body wanted to do was crash into a heap on the floor. He willed himself to stand.

Inside the carcer, Richard decided to meditate on God. He prayed as he reflected on his faith. Before long, he began to repeat the phrase "Jesus, dear Bridegroom of my soul, I love You" over and over again. At first it felt strange repeating the phrase to himself again and again, but he kept at it. He repeated the words in time to his heartbeat. Before long, the words lost their significance. They became a sound activity that occupied part of his conscious mind while the rest of his mind seemed to stop functioning and drift away, detached from the reality of where he was.

The practice worked so well that the two days Richard spent standing in the carcer seemed to go by quickly. He was not even aware of consciously holding himself rigid and erect on his feet the whole time.

Not long after the experience in the carcer, the prisoners' toilets were blocked, and Richard was permitted to use one of the guards' toilets. In this room there was a mirror on the wall. Richard stared into it. Looking back at him was an old man, gaunt and pale, with yellow-tinged eyes. Richard stepped back from the mirror startled. This was the first time he had seen himself in over a year, and he had aged twenty years in that time.

Time passed slowly locked in his quiet, solitary cell seeing nobody but his guard. Yet Richard looked forward to passing the time hearing news from around the various dungeon cells. By now it seemed as if most of the prisoners had learned Morse code and were willing to pass along jokes, words of encouragement, and information. And even though Richard was not being actively interrogated, the dread of it always loomed over him.

Then one day Richard was taken from his cell and introduced to Lieutenant Grecu, a self-assured young interrogator. The lieutenant asked Richard all sorts of questions, trying to get him to admit that the funds he had distributed on behalf of the World Council of Churches had really been used for spying. Richard refuted the argument and was then returned to his cell.

The next day, an hour after the sounding of the morning bell, Richard was again taken to Lieutenant Grecu's office. The lieutenant sat holding a rubber truncheon in his hand. Richard assumed he was about to be beaten once more. Instead, Lieutenant Grecu looked at him and shouted, "Your story yesterday was all lies." Then, standing up, he pushed a sheet of paper and a pen across the desk to Richard. "You have been communicating in code with other prisoners. This we know. I want to know exactly what each of them said to you. And I want to know any other breach of prison rules you have participated in. Write it all on the paper. Tell me the truth this time. I will be back in half an hour," he said, banging the truncheon hard on the desk before leaving the room.

A bright light bulb shone overhead as Richard picked up the pen. It wasn't easy to write at first, since he hadn't used a pen in over a year.

Sure enough, Lieutenant Grecu walked back into the room a half hour later, swinging his rubber truncheon. "Let me see what you've written," he said, taking the paper from Richard and sitting down at his desk to read it. Richard watched as the lieutenant's eyes scanned the shaky handwriting, and he wondered what the lieutenant's reaction would be. On the paper Richard had admitted to breaking the rules and that he had tapped the gospel through the walls to other prisoners. He said he didn't know the names of the other prisoners but noted that he had never spoken against the Communists. As a Christian, he noted, he was to love his enemies, to understand them, and to pray for their conversion. The last sentence he wrote said, "I can give no statement about what others said to me, for a priest of God can never be a witness for the prosecution. My calling is to defend, not to accuse."

"Mr. Wurmbrand, why do you say you love me?" Lieutenant Grecu asked when he had read Richard's statement. "This is one of the Christian commandments no one can keep. I could not love someone who imprisoned me for years and starved and tortured me."

"It's not just keeping a commandment," Richard replied. "When I became a Christian, I was reborn with a new character, full of love. Just as only water flows from a spring, so only love flows from a loving heart."

Lieutenant Grecu looked at Richard and began asking him more questions about his faith. The two of them talked for hours, focusing on the relationship of Christianity to Marxist doctrine. Richard pointed out that the first book Karl Marx wrote was a commentary on the Gospel of John and that in the preface to *Das Kapital* Marx had noted that Christianity, especially Protestant Christianity, was the ideal religion for the renewal of lives made wretched by sin. The atheistic lieutenant was surprised by this.

"Since my life had been made wretched by sin, I was simply following Marx's advice when I became a Christian," Richard added.

The next day Richard was taken back to Lieutenant Grecu's office for another long discussion about Christianity. Soon this became a daily occurrence. During one of these long discussions, the lieutenant reiterated that he was an atheist. Richard explained that *atheism* was a holy word for Christians. When the early Christians were thrown to the lions for their faith, they were called 'atheists' by Emperors Nero and Caligula, he further explained.

"Christians don't criticize the Communist Party for atheism but for producing the wrong kind of atheists," Richard told the lieutenant, going on to explain that there were two kinds of atheists: those who say that there is no God and therefore they can do all the evil they like; and those atheists who say that since there is no God, they must do all the good that God would do if He existed. "When Jesus saw men hungry and sick," Richard said, "He took the whole responsibility of caring for them upon Himself. And that is how we know that Jesus was God." Then looking his interrogator in the eye, Richard added, "If you become that sort of atheist, Lieutenant, loving and serving everyone, men will soon discover that you have become a son of God, and you will discover the godhead in you."

Richard's words stunned Lieutenant Grecu into silence.

Two weeks passed before Richard was taken back to the lieutenant's office, at which time Lieutenant Grecu told him he had thought a lot about their last conversation and now wanted to become a Christian. He confessed his sins to Richard and told him he would do all he could to help the prisoners, even though it would be dangerous. Over the next several weeks, Lieutenant Grecu did just that. Then one day he disappeared. One of the guards told Richard he had been arrested.

The interrogations continued after the disappearance of Lieutenant Grecu. This time his interrogators tried a new tactic. They injected Richard with drugs that made him weepy and sick. After each interrogation, Richard's health slipped a little. His hair stopped growing, and his fingernails became strangely spongy. It was hard for Richard to stand, and he was beginning to cough up blood. Richard knew that his tuberculosis had returned.

One afternoon someone different peered through the grill on the cell door. An hour later two soldiers came and carried Richard away. Richard was barely conscious and didn't know whether they were taking him to a grave or to another prison. The soldiers carried him up the two flights of stairs and outside. For the first time in nearly three years, Richard saw the moon and stars shining overhead and breathed in fresh air. He could hear the sound of traffic, a distant siren, and a dog barking. As he was loaded into an ambulance and driven off, it was almost too much for him to take in.

Richard looked out the ambulance window at the tops of buildings. He recognized many of them against the night sky. They drove up a hill, and Richard knew where they were—Vacaresti, the magnificent eighteenth-century monastery now used as a prison.

The ambulance door swung open, and a guard wrapped a towel around Richard's head so he couldn't see. Richard felt himself being half-carried, half-dragged from the ambulance. He stumbled up a flight of stairs, relieved that he wasn't going underground again. He was pushed onto a bed, and the towel covering his head was removed. Richard looked around. He was in another tiny cell, but his heart filled with joy. The cell had a window he could see out of. Perhaps he would catch a glimpse of a bird or even a rainbow when the sun came up. "Only the doctor is allowed to see this man—no one else," he heard one guard tell the other.

When the one guard left, the other guard said to him, "So what have you done to deserve such harsh treatment?"

"I'm a pastor, a child of God," Richard replied.

The guard leaned in and said in a low voice, "Praise God. I'm a believer too. My name is Tachici."

Tears welled up in Richard's eyes. "God is good. He has His people everywhere," he said.

"I will help you all I can," Tachici replied.

Over the following week, Richard's physical condition deteriorated. He was often delirious and vomited up any food he managed to swallow. Yet he was grateful to be at Vacaresti. The cells had thinner walls, and when he was conscious, Richard was able to get to know the prisoners to the right and the left of him. The guards did not insist on total silence. Richard enjoyed interesting conversations with the other prisoners.

Two weeks after his arrival, with a towel once again wrapped around his head, Richard was taken from the cell. This time he ended up in a large room filled with sunlight. Four men and a woman sat on one side of a table, and a single chair was on the other side. The guard pulled Richard over to it. By now

Richard's vision was blurred, and he had been suffering from a high fever for several days. The man in the middle on the other side of the table looked at Richard. "This is your trial. A lawyer has been appointed to represent you. He has waived your right to bring witnesses. Sit down. Let the trial begin," he announced.

Richard struggled to concentrate as he slipped in and out of consciousness. Two guards held him down while another gave him an injection. His mind became clearer. The trial was under way. His lawyer was talking. The woman was talking. The man in the middle was talking. Richard struggled hard to make sense of what they said. Apparently he was a spy who had been paid by the World Council of Churches. Richard felt himself slump. He was given another injection.

"Have you anything to say?" the man in the middle asked.

Did he have anything to say? What could he say? What did they want him to say? What did God want him to say? Only three words came out of his mouth: "I love God."

"Twenty years' hard labor," the man in the middle bellowed.

The towel was once more wrapped around Richard's head, and he was dragged back to his cell. He had been away just ten minutes.

Two days later, another guard arrived at the cell door with another towel. This time Richard was too weak to walk. The guard picked him up and carried him away.

Richard felt himself being placed on wet cobblestones. Then a metal ring was clamped around his ankle. He felt the thud of a hammer against the metal. It could only mean one thing—he was being fitted with a leg iron, chain, and weight.

The towel was removed, and Richard, along with the fifty-pound weight attached to his ankle, was lifted into the back of a truck with other prisoners also in leg irons. Richard wondered where they were taking him this time. Surely anyone could see that he was too sick to start his twenty years of hard labor.

Chapter 12

Walking Out Alive

It was dark by the time the truck pulled to a halt. Richard and some of the other prisoners were transferred from the back of the truck into a boxcar. When it was full, the door slammed shut. Soon a whistle blew, and the boxcar jerked as the train pulled away from the siding. Richard remembered the stories he had heard about how the Nazis rounded up Jews and sent them in trains to concentration camps and certain death. Did that same fate await him?

The train rattled and creaked along the track, leaving the plains and ascending into the Carpathian Mountains. Along the way, Richard realized that he and the other men inside the boxcar all had one thing in common—they were all suffering from tuberculosis, or TB. He was not surprised when the train hissed to a stop in the town of Tirgul-Ocna, 175 miles north of Bucharest, where there was a prison sanatorium. The town was less than a hundred miles from Noua, the small village where Richard had convalesced during his first bout of TB. That was where Christian Wolfkes had given him his first Bible. How Richard wished he had that Bible with him now.

After the grueling train trip, Richard was so weak he couldn't walk at all. He and his fifty-pound leg weight were loaded into a cart with six other sick prisoners and pulled by hand through the town to the sanatorium. When he arrived, his leg iron, chain, and weight were removed. Richard was relieved. Then his spirits soared when he saw Dr. Aldea, a member of his old congregation, waiting to check the new arrivals. Richard and the six other men from the cart were placed in a room together.

"It's wonderful to see you again, Richard," Dr. Aldea said as he leaned in to take Richard's pulse. "I have to tell you, I'm a prisoner too. They let me examine prisoners because they're so short of personnel, but the Communist doctor is the one who makes all the decisions. He will say what becomes of you."

The following week the Communist doctor examined Richard and declared he needed to be reassigned to Room 4. Two of the prisoners who had arrived with Richard had already been sent there.

"It is not good news," Dr. Aldea said kindly. "To be honest, I would think you have about two weeks to live. Your lungs are pitted with cavities—they're like a sponge—and you're getting weaker every day.

If only we had medicine. I do believe a new type of medicine has been developed in America for TB, but our government calls that propaganda, so we do not have it."

"Why Room 4?" Richard asked.

"That is where men go to live out their last days," the doctor responded.

That afternoon two prisoners, who were also TB patients, carried Richard along a corridor to the infamous Room 4. Twelve beds were arranged in the room in two rows, and a row of windows, which were all open, allowed fresh air to pour inside. Outside Richard could see some of the prisoners tending a vegetable patch. He soon learned that this was a different kind of prison. Everyone in it had TB, and since it was such a contagious disease, few guards and no nurses were inside the building. The prisoners did everything for themselves and, in the case of those who were too sick, for each other.

Lying on a pallet with a single filthy blanket over him, Richard was soon one of the sickest men in Room 4. He was unconscious most of the time, which he was grateful for. His chest and back ached, and his body was covered with pus-filled boils.

After a few weeks in Room 4, Richard began to feel a little stronger and remained conscious a little longer. Dr. Aldea could not account for it. "It is a miracle," he said. "Your lungs should not be operating." But they were. Month after month Richard held on in the Death Room. He watched other men being brought in alive and carried out dead. Some of them were college professors who contradicted Communist ideology, others were priests, and then there was a wave of farmers who arrived at the sanatorium prison. The farmers had been moved off their land to make way for the establishment of large state-owned farms that were supposed to produce an abundance of produce for the Romanian people.

Richard saw little of this promised abundance in prison. There were no medicines, no sheets on the beds, and scant food to eat. Still, they did have one thing they prized in Room 4—the freedom to speak their minds. Since it was assumed that no one was going to leave the room alive, men felt liberated to have honest conversations with each other.

That all changed, however, when a "reeducation program" was introduced to the prison. Since few guards were inside, the authorities armed the "best Communists," about a quarter of all the prisoners, with rubber truncheons and told them to punish anyone who was not a Communist. Mayhem followed as the new "trustees" zealously went about their business. Richard had never before witnessed such cruelty among men. Their actions led him to despair.

Just when he thought he could no longer take the brutality around him, a new prisoner arrived in Room 4. Avram Radonovici, a former music critic, had brought with him two incredible gifts. One was his ability to entertain everyone in the room by humming long melodies by Mozart, Beethoven, and Bach. The other was even better. Because he had tuberculosis of the spine, much of Avram's body was in a plaster cast. The night he arrived, he put his hand down the side of the cast and pulled out a small book. It was the Gospel of John.

"I dropped it down my cast when the police came for me in my home," Avram said with glee. "They brought me straight here and didn't think to check if I'd tucked anything away."

Richard sat transfixed. It had been over three and a half years since he had seen a Bible, or any book, for that matter.

"Would you like to borrow it?" Avram asked.

Tears of joy rolled down Richard's cheeks as he took the book in his hands, thanking God under his breath for it. Over the next several weeks, many prisoners learned the entire Gospel of John by heart. And away from the prying eyes of the trustees, Richard taught Bible studies to the dying men.

Each new prisoner in Room 4 brought with him some kind of news. One man told Richard he had heard that Sabina was alive but had been sent to work in a forced labor camp on the dreaded Canal Project, which was supposed to link the Danube River with the Black Sea. But there was no news of what had become of Mihai. Richard prayed that his wife would survive her ordeal.

In early March 1953, the prisoners heard church bells tolling in the distance. They soon learned that the bells were ringing to mark the death of Joseph Stalin, the brutal leader of the Soviet Union. Few in the prison were sad, though they all wondered what would happen next. What kind of turn would

Communism take now that Stalin was dead? Would the new Russian leader loosen the control of the Soviet Union over Romania? The prisoners pondered the possibility that they would all be let out of prison at last. They didn't have to wait long for an answer.

An investigator from the Legal Department in Bucharest came to inspect the Tirgul-Ocna Prison. He even came into Room 4 during his inspection. Soon afterward the prison commandant was replaced, the brutal treatment of prisoners tapered off, and prisoners were given a little more food to eat. However, no one was released from prison.

Richard stayed in Room 4, outliving everyone who had been there when he arrived, as well as the many others who had been brought to the room since his arrival. In spring 1954, the prison doctor ordered Richard to return to a regular cell. After two and a half years in Room 4, Richard no longer appeared to be dying. He was the first patient to walk out of Room 4—the Death Room—alive. All the others had been carried out wrapped in sheets for burial.

Something else amazing happened at this time. The prisoners were allowed to begin receiving monthly parcels from their families. Richard wasn't sure what had become of his home in Bucharest, but he mailed a postcard there anyway, asking that he be sent food, cigarettes, and "Doctor Filon's old clothes." Although Richard didn't smoke, he had discovered that offering a prisoner a cigarette was an effective way of starting a meaningful conversation with him. Doctor Filon's old clothes was a code he hoped his family would understand. He was not allowed to ask for medicine to be sent to him, not even something to relieve the excruciating pain of a toothache he was suffering from. He hoped that someone at home would figure out that he wanted medicine sent to him.

Then one day, much to Richard's astonishment, a parcel arrived for him. As he unwrapped it, to his delight, not only were the things he had asked for in the package, but also someone had understood his code and tucked inside the package one hundred grams of streptomycin, the antibiotic Dr. Aldea had told him about that was being used in the West to treat TB. The package also contained a letter from Mihai. Richard read it anxiously, and then joy flooded over him when he read that Sabina had been freed from the labor camp and was now in Bucharest with Mihai. Sabina could not leave the city, or the authorities would have her arrested again. The two of them lived together in two small rooms in the attic of the old mission building.

As Richard looked at the streptomycin, he knew what he would do with it. It seemed to him that he didn't need it. In what even the Communist doctor was calling a miracle, the disease that was supposed to kill him had not. But there were men in Room 4 whose lives might be saved by taking the drug, so he handed it over for someone else to use.

Then in January 1955, Richard received remarkable news. Mihai had been given permission to visit him in prison. Richard had last seen his son seven years before, when Mihai was nine years old. Now his son was sixteen, having just celebrated his birthday. He wondered what Mihai would look like and, given the state of Richard's health, whether Mihai would even recognize his own father.

At last the day of the visit arrived. Richard was led into a large room with a rounded ceiling, making it look like the inside of a tunnel, and was told to sit in a box at one end of the room. A narrow window with three iron bars across it opened from the box to the room. Richard sat in the box and stared into the room, a guard at his side. "Mihai Wurmbrand," he heard another guard shout. Richard took a deep breath and waited. And then his son appeared, sitting on the other side of the narrow window. He had grown tall and lean over the intervening years. He was pale and hollow-cheeked, and above his upper lip was the beginning of a moustache. All Richard wanted to do was hug his son, but that was not permitted. Instead, the two of them stared into each other's eyes for a moment. "It is good to see you, Son. You have grown," Richard began. "Tell me, how is your mother."

"Mother says to tell you that even if you die in prison, you must not be sad, because we will all meet in paradise."

Richard wasn't sure how to respond. Should he laugh or cry? How he wanted to see Sabina again. "And do you have food at home?" he asked.

"Mother is well again after her experience in the labor camp. And yes, we have food. Our Father is very rich," Mihai said.

The guard monitoring Richard's conversation chuckled at this. Mihai had been referring to God when he said "Father," but Richard supposed the guard interpreted it that the authorities had finally convinced his wife to divorce him and now she was remarried.

Richard asked his son more questions, but he could tell that Mihai was nervous and replied to many of his questions with Bible verses. All too soon, the visit was over, and Mihai was being led from the room. Before being escorted away, he told Richard he had left him a parcel containing food and some other supplies with the guards at the prison gate.

Richard watched Mihai leave the room before the guard led him away. He hadn't really learned a lot from his son, and he had so many questions he wanted to ask, but he knew it was forbidden to do so. Still, after seven years, it was good to see his son again and know that Sabina was healthy and safe.

Sadly, the visits, parcels, and letters from families did not last, and the old restrictions against such things were reinstated. But Richard was thankful he'd had the chance to see Mihai.

In March 1955, Richard turned forty-six, though his prison experience made his body feel like he was turning eighty.

More and more prisoners with TB began to arrive at Tirgul-Ocna, and beds for them were in short supply. In June 1955, Richard was named among a group of prisoners to be transferred to another prison. Dr. Aldea disagreed with the decision, but he could do nothing about it. "You're not fit to be moved," he told

Richard, "but they will not listen to me. Please, take care of yourself. And if you get any more streptomycin. Use it on yourself. Do not give it away."

On the day of his departure from Tirgul-Ocna, Richard was led out to the prison yard. He stepped forward when his name was called to have a leg iron, chain, and weight fitted to his ankle for transport.

For the next year Richard was shunted from prison to prison, first to Craiova Prison, 140 miles away in the southwest of the country, then to the same labor camp in Cernavoda where Sabina had been held as she was forced to work on the now-abandoned Canal Project. From there he was taken north to Gherla in Transylvania, and after that he was sent back to Vacaresti, where he had been taken after his release from solitary confinement in the dungeon of Uranus Prison.

From Vacaresti Richard was sent on to Jilava Prison, a notoriously damp and unhealthy prison near Bucharest. This prison was built to hold five hundred prisoners, but two thousand were crowded into it. With each new move, Richard felt his strength ebbing. Things became a blur. He could barely remember where he was. He forgot how to say the Lord's Prayer, and Bible stories fused with other traditional stories men told each other. At times he feared he was losing his mind, but he continued to pray as best he could.

One day at mealtime in Jilava Prison while he ate his bowl of watery carrot soup, Richard sat on the bunk of a neighboring prisoner. The prisoner explained to him that he was a radio engineer who had been imprisoned for passing on information to the West. When he learned that Richard was a pastor, he told him, "I was brought to Christ through my knowledge of Morse code. It happened about five years ago. I was in a dungeon cell at Uranus Prison, where I was being interrogated. While I was there, an unknown pastor was in the cell next door. I taught him how to tap Morse code, and then he tapped Bible verses to me through the wall."

Tears welled up in Richard's eyes as he looked at the man. "I was that pastor," he told him. The two of them became instant allies and together shared the gospel with other prisoners.

During this time, news filtered through to the prisoners that Nikita Khrushchev, the new leader of the Soviet Union, had openly denounced Joseph Stalin as a murderer and a tyrant. Many of those who had supported Stalin had been imprisoned, and a number of supporters had been executed. In Romania a process had begun to discredit Stalin. Already some political prisoners imprisoned under Stalin's influence were being given amnesty and being released from jail.

Richard, like the other prisoners in Jilava, wondered if he might soon be released.

He tried to imagine himself a free man, but it was impossible. What would Sabina look like now? And what about Mihai? Had he been able to find work as the son of a prisoner, or was he in prison himself? Richard had so many questions and so few answers. Then one morning a guard came to his cell and ordered, "Interrogation at once. Move, now!"

Richard followed the guard along the prison corridors and out across the prison yard. Then the prison gate was unlocked, and Richard stepped through it. Outside, a prison clerk handed him a sheet of paper with a court order printed on it saying that under amnesty he was now a free man. "But I've served only eight and a half years of my twenty-year sentence," Richard told the clerk.

"You must leave at once. Don't argue. Get out," the clerk ordered.

Jilava Prison sat three miles outside Bucharest. Richard set off walking across the fields toward the city. It was hard for him to fathom that he was free. He was dirty and dressed in patched pants and a ragged shirt. He wondered if people would think he had escaped and call the police to come and arrest him. As he walked, he let the tall grass run across his hands. He stopped from time to time to touch the bark on tree trunks. He had never imagined that such simple actions could feel so good.

An old couple approached him as he waded through the grass. "Have you come from there?" they asked, pointing toward the prison. Richard nodded. The man pulled a coin from his pocket and gave it to Richard. A little farther on, a woman asked if he had come from the prison. Once again Richard acknowledged he had, and she too gave him a coin.

When Richard had crossed the fields and reached the outskirts of Bucharest, more people approached him. It was obvious he had come from the prison, and they asked about friends or family members who were imprisoned there. Richard told them what he knew. When at last he reached a tram stop, where he planned to use one of the coins to buy a ticket, the tram operator let him ride for free. As the tram rumbled across the city, a woman with a basket of strawberries sat down beside him. He looked at the strawberries longingly, and the woman gave him some to eat. No strawberry had ever tasted so good to Richard, after having eaten wretched slop for eight and a half years.

When the tram reached his stop, Richard climbed off and walked toward the old mission building. He stopped at the door of the building and thought about the last time he had crossed its threshold. It had been a brisk, sunny Sunday morning eight and a half years before when he had left the building to take a stroll before church. And now he had returned home. He hoped his wife and son were still living there.

Chapter 13

"You Won't Preach Again"

Richard opened the building door and stepped inside. Several teenagers stood in the hallway. Among them was a tall, dark-haired young man who let out a yell. "Father! Is it really you, Father?"

Opening his arms, Richard gave his son the hug he had wanted to give him a year and a half before when Mihai visited him in prison. The other teenagers gathered around, crying and shouting with joy and excitement.

When the commotion died down, Mihai explained how he and his mother lived in two rooms in the attic. Richard knew the rooms well. He and Sabina had once used them for storage when they lived in their second-floor apartment. One room was about twelve by fifteen feet, and the other around twelve by nine feet. Mihai pointed out that the rest of the old mission building was occupied by various families from the church.

Sabina was visiting friends, so Mihai guided Richard upstairs to the attic to wait for her. When they reached the family's living quarters, Richard looked around the two rooms. Mihai slept in the smaller room, and Sabina and Janetta slept on a broken sofa in the other room. Janetta was a Christian woman who helped Sabina run the underground church. In these two small rooms the three slept, lived, and cooked. The attic had no heating, and Richard noticed an enamel bowl sitting on the floor to catch drips that leaked through the roof.

As news spread that Pastor Wurmbrand was home, a crowd began to make its way up the stairs to the attic. When Sabina arrived home, Richard stared at her. She was more beautiful than he remembered. Her hair was now streaked with gray, and her face was thin but radiant. "Before we embrace," Richard told his wife, "there is something you must understand. You must not think I have been despondent for the past eight and a half years. I come from my family in prison, where there were many joys, to my family here." With that, he reached out and kissed Sabina and held her.

As Richard and Sabina hugged, people continued to flow into their small rooms. For the rest of the day and well into the night, people ascended the stairs to the attic to welcome Richard back. Because there was enough room for only a few people at a time in the two rooms, some had to leave when others arrived.

Around midnight, the crowd had dwindled to just Richard, Sabina, Mihai, and Janetta. It was time to sleep.

A neighbor had brought up a mattress for Richard, and they padded the end of it with a cushion to accommodate his long body. Richard lay down, but he couldn't sleep. He had so much to think about. His wife and son were safe. He was free. Although the walls of the attic were moldy and a bowl sat on the floor to catch leaks, it was home. He was safe. He was sure that when he awoke he wouldn't arise to more beatings and interrogation.

The following morning Richard and Mihai took a walk in the park. It made Richard a little nervous to be outside with so much open space and no guards in sight. But there was beauty all around—a butterfly, red flowering trees, moss-covered rocks. Everything seemed vibrant and alive. As they walked, Mihai asked Richard what he had learned while in prison.

Richard thought it an excellent question, one he'd had over eight years to think about. "You know I had no Bible in prison," he began. "For a while I had a portion of the Gospel of John, but that was taken away. I have forgotten much of it. Last night I tried to find the book of Daniel in a Bible, but I could not, and it used to be my favorite book. But that doesn't matter. I may have forgotten all of my theology, but there are five things I will never forget."

"What are they, Father?"

"The first is that God is alive and He is our loving Father. The second is that Jesus Christ is our Savior, and the third is that the Holy Spirit is at work within us to make us more like Christ. The fourth is that I have no question in my mind that there is eternal life."

"And the fifth?" Mihai asked.

Richard reached out and put his hand on his son's shoulder. "Ah, the last thing I know for sure is that love is the best way. Whatever happens, love is the best way to respond. That's what I learned in prison."

During the walk Mihai caught Richard up on the last eight and a half years of his life. During the three years that Sabina was in the prison work camp, he lived with Alice, an elderly woman who had been a Sunday school teacher in the church. Because he was the son of a political prisoner, Mihai had not been able to attend school. Instead, he had studied any way he could and felt he had learned enough to pass the high school graduation exams if he were ever given the chance.

An old church member helped Mihai get a job as an assistant piano tuner for the Bucharest Orchestra. Mihai was fired when the orchestra leader learned who his father was. But during his time with the orchestra, Mihai had garnered enough skill to carry on afterward tuning pianos in private homes. He didn't make much money doing so, and what he made went toward buying food.

Mihai told Richard he had read many of the old books and sermons he had written. They had been stored in a secret room in the basement of the mission building. "After reading them, I can say I love you very much, but you're you and I'm me. I'm not exactly like you. I don't think like you in many ways," Mihai said.

At first Richard was taken aback. In prison he had imagined telling Mihai Bible stories and singing hymns with him, but he hadn't imagined that Mihai might come to different conclusions about things. Then Richard smiled. In prison, time seemed to stand still. Somehow he continued to imagine Mihai to be the nine-year-old boy he was when he was arrested. But his son was now a young man who had formed his own opinions. "Truly," Richard said, "I'm glad you say that, because to own your personality is to receive one of God's greatest gifts to mankind."

Mihai explained that since the government forbade him to go to school, he had sat in the attic rooms hour after hour, day after day, reading all sorts of books. Richard thought back to when he was ten years old in Istanbul and his father had died. He attended school off and on, but as Mihai had done, he preferred to stay at home and learn by reading books from the library his father had amassed before his death.

By the time their walk was over, Mihai had to help Richard climb the stairs. Several old church members were waiting for him. Richard lay on his mattress as he spoke with them. The walk had exhausted him.

"You really need to go to the hospital to be checked out," Sabina told Richard after the visitors had left. "It's a miracle you survived at all, but you're so very weak."

Richard hated to leave home so soon after returning from prison, but he knew that Sabina was right. He did need medical attention.

The doctor at the local hospital examined Richard and discovered that his lungs were covered with scars where the tuberculous infection had healed. (The doctor could not say definitively how the healing had happened.) Lasting damage had been done to his body from the rounds of torture. The doctor counted eighteen marks on Richard's body—burns, scars from lashings, and indentations from being hit with hammers and truncheons. After the examination, Richard was admitted to the hospital until he grew stronger.

Word soon got around that Pastor Wurmbrand was a patient in the hospital, and people began slipping in and out of his room at all hours of the day and night. They wanted to see him with their own eyes, and they wanted prayer for their loved ones or information about family members in prison. Before long the crowds grew so large that Richard was transferred to another hospital so that he would not attract the attention of the Securitate.

Sabina visited and sat with him for hours every day. During these times she gradually told Richard about the painful things she and Mihai had been through since Richard's arrest. She told him how she had been arrested by the Securitate in August 1950, two and a half years after his arrest. She had been taken to Cernavoda on the Danube River, where she was put to work on the excavation of what the prisoners called the "canalul morţii"—the death canal—an immense slave-labor project in which tens of thousands of political prisoners worked to dig from Cernavoda to the Black Sea port of Constanţa. If completed, the 40-mile-long canal was supposed to cut off 250 miles of winding and unstable waterways between the Black Sea and inland Eastern Europe. Sabina told Richard about how the working conditions were terrible and how the political prisoners were worked to death. No one knew how many people died, and when forced laborers on the project ran low, the Communist government would round up more "socially unacceptable" people to take the place of those who had died, until they too were worked to death.

Richard had no idea how Sabina, so petite and delicate, had survived. She told him that two of her ribs were broken when some guards decided to throw her into the frigid Danube River for amusement. But for some reason, when she was too weak for the canal project, instead of working her to death, they sent her to work on a collective farm before releasing her without explanation in early 1953.

The Securitate now kept a file on her and called her into their office from time to time. They had also pressed her to divorce Richard, saying she could have a work permit if she was no longer the wife of a political prisoner. But she refused to divorce her husband.

Sabina also told Richard about her work with the underground church. With so many pastors, including Richard, having been imprisoned, the women, Sabina among them, stepped forward to lead the church. All over Bucharest and across the country, small groups of Christians met in secret for church. Because there were so few pastors, the sectarian boundaries between denominations fell away. Catholics, Orthodox Christians, Lutherans, and many others all met together, focusing on the basic elements of the Christian faith.

Sabina said the underground church resembled the early church written about in the New Testament.

These small church meetings were held in basements, attics, houses, fields, even forests. Often people arriving at a meeting had to give a secret knock to be let in. Sabina said they had to be careful, since spies for the Securitate were everywhere, trying to infiltrate their meetings. As a result, more than a few leaders in the underground church had been arrested and thrown in jail for their activities.

The issue of spies with the church had perplexed Sabina, and she began thinking about using the Communists' methods against them. She and Janetta read *What Is to Be Done,* a pamphlet written by Vladimir Lenin, leader of Russia's Communist Revolution, and published in 1902. The book laid out Lenin's plan for conquering the world with Communism. One of the first principles he laid out was the need to infiltrate rival organizations. Sabina remembered how quickly Communists had infiltrated seminaries and the clergy after the Soviet Union took control of Romania.

Inspired by the principle of infiltration, Sabina and Janetta came up with a dangerous plan, which they kept secret. They approached only young people who they knew had the character and depth of faith necessary to pay lip service to Communism while spying on Communists for the good of Christ and His church in Romania.

Several people took up the challenge. Among them was Trudi, an attractive girl from a country town. Sabina told Richard how Trudi secured a job helping in the home of Colonel Shircanu, who worked with the Securitate. After only a month of working in the colonel's house, Trudi sent a message to Sabina and

Janetta that a particular pastor attending the underground meetings had agreed to spy for the Secret Police. Sabina and several other leaders in the underground church challenged the pastor. He admitted his crime and quickly left Bucharest for the countryside. Trudi also alerted them to other spies.

With a smile on her face, Sabina told Richard they had even held church meetings in Colonel Shircanu's home when he and his family vacationed in the countryside. And since the family seemed to take many vacations, the colonel's house was now a regular meeting place.

Sabina also explained that while organizing the underground church, she had eked out a living for herself and Mihai by sewing and knitting garments. She had even attempted to raise silkworms she had found in a local cemetery. Richard was impressed with his wife's fearlessness and tenacity, as well as her resourcefulness, in the face of persecution.

By the time Richard and Sabina's twentieth wedding anniversary rolled around on October 26, 1956, Richard's strength had returned. He had been released from the hospital and was back living in the attic with his family. The life he and Sabina now shared was different from anything they could have imagined when they married. Since they had no money to spare, Richard found a blank notebook in which he wrote poems to Sabina. She cried when he gave it to her for their anniversary.

With the denunciation of Joseph Stalin by Nikita Khrushchev, the Romanian government made some concessions to Christian churches. They gave several denominations, among them Lutherans, permission to operate legally, though always under the control of the government. Many Christians in the underground church referred to these government-allowed churches as "show churches," intended to show the outside world that Romania's Communist government didn't really persecute Christians. Through Bishop Muller, leader of the state-sanctioned Lutheran Church, Richard was granted a license to preach.

The bishop was an old friend of Richard's. He explained that while he was head of a show church and made it look as if he were following the government's rules, he was deeply committed to the well-being of Christians in Romania. He told Richard that he carried on a parallel but secret ministry among underground Christians. Richard was impressed by his old friend's commitment and accepted the position in the Lutheran Church, intending to mirror the bishop's approach.

As a sign of their concession to churches, the government also allowed a small theological seminary to be established at Sibiu, about 170 miles northwest of Bucharest. Mihai told Richard he wanted to study at the new seminary. Richard knew that the true gospel would not be taught there and was concerned that Mihai's faith would be eroded. All he could do was pray for his son.

The fees for the seminary were expensive, set high by the government to discourage people from seeking a theological education. Bishop Muller, who helped set up the seminary, offered to support Mihai financially. He also reassured Richard that while there would be government spies and informants there, and Mihai would have to endure Communist indoctrination classes, the seminary's professors were well-qualified men determined to give their students the best theological education possible under the circumstances.

Following Mihai's departure to seminary, Richard, who had spent a lot of time reading and studying to fill in the prison-induced gaps in his memories, was asked to give a one-week lecture series at Cluj University. At the first lecture on Monday, fifty students showed up to hear Richard speak. At his last lecture on Friday, one thousand students attended.

Among the crowd was Comrade Rugojanu, an official with the Ministry of Cults. Richard had expected someone from the Ministry of Cults to be keeping an eye on him. It was best to assume that someone acting as a spy was listening to you wherever you were. The last point Richard spoke on during his Friday lecture was hope. "The wheel of life," he said, "may put the emperor's physician in prison, but it goes on turning. Who knows? That same physician may one day be back in the palace, even sitting on the throne."

Richard attended a meeting of Lutheran pastors the next day. During the meeting Comrade Rugojanu stormed into the room. "What are you doing here? Trying to make excuses for what you preached yesterday. Well, it won't work," he said, glaring at Richard.

"What didn't you like about my message?" Richard asked.

"You said the wheel is always turning, but you're wrong, very wrong. I know you were talking about Communists falling from power, but it will not happen. The wheel will not turn again. Communism is forever!" the comrade said, his voice rising to a shout.

"But I said nothing about Communism," Richard replied. "I was talking about the wheel of life. It keeps changing. Sometimes things go your way, and sometimes they don't."

Comrade Rugojanu's face turned a deep shade of red. "You're finished, Wurmbrand. Finished! You cannot control yourself. You are not to preach like that. I will have your license revoked. Mark my words, you won't preach again."

Before the next week was over, Comrade Rugojanu had called a meeting of government-sanctioned church leaders to denounce Richard, whose license to preach was then officially revoked. He had held the license for six weeks. Of course, Richard had no intention of giving up preaching or pastoring and caring for Christians. He would just do it underground, out of the glare of the Ministry of Cults and its henchmen.

Richard joined Sabina in helping lead the underground church. Together they comforted the sick and dying and encouraged those who had lost hope to keep their eyes on God. "The wheel will turn again," Richard told them. "Hold on to the promises of God. He is good." Richard preached and taught from the Bible at the various underground church groups that met wherever and whenever they could, often right under the noses of the unsuspecting Communist officials.

As 1958 progressed, Richard began to sense the net closing in on him. He felt sure it wouldn't be long before he was arrested once more. He was right. Early in the morning on January 15, 1959, two years and six months after Richard had been released from prison, he and Sabina awoke to a terrific noise. The door of their attic room flew open, and the light was switched on. Several policemen rushed in. "Are you Richard Wurmbrand?" one of them asked.

"Yes," Richard replied, swinging his legs over the side of the bed.

The captain of the police squad pulled Richard to his feet and said to him, "Get in the other room."

Richard was pushed into the room and handcuffed. He could hear the police dumping the contents of the cupboards and his desk onto the floor in his bedroom. He sat on the end of Mihai's empty bed, grateful that his son was away at seminary.

After what seemed like an eternity, the police captain came into the room. "Time to go," he said, grabbing Richard by the shoulders and guiding him back into his bedroom.

Sabina stood there eyeing the captain. "Aren't you ashamed to treat innocent people like this?" she asked.

The captain ignored her and pushed Richard toward the door. Instead, Richard lunged toward Sabina. "I won't leave this house without a struggle unless you unlock these handcuffs and let me embrace my wife," Richard demanded.

The captain nodded. "Let him go," he ordered.

Richard took Sabina's hand, and together they knelt beside their bed as they had done so many times before. Richard prayed that God would be with them both and protect them until they saw each other again. He also prayed for Mihai. Sabina then began singing a hymn, and Richard joined in. When the hymn was over, the police captain looked at Richard with tears in his eyes. "It's time to go," he said gently.

Richard nodded. He stood and hugged Sabina. He was once more handcuffed and led down the stairs and out into the freezing night. "Give my love to Mihai," Richard yelled to Sabina as the door of the waiting van opened and he was shoved inside.

Chapter 14

"We Thought You Were Dead"

Richard stared up at the banner on the far wall. It read, "Justice for the People in the Service of the People." He was sitting in a small, drab room before a judge dressed in a military uniform. Two weeks had passed since he was dragged from his bed by police in the early morning. In that time, he had been beaten, mocked, and starved.

Richard chose to focus on the positive. Sabina and Mihai were both there in the room, sitting right in front of him. He kept his eyes on them, hoping to fix their faces in his mind for the future.

Two officials flanked Richard as he sat waiting for the proceeding to begin. At last the first official stood and gave a speech about the reason Richard had been arrested. He had, apparently, committed various crimes, though no specifics were given. The names of people who supposedly saw him committing these crimes against the state were read, though Richard didn't recognize any of them.

Then the second official stood. Richard realized that this man was the attorney who would defend him against the alleged crimes. Richard had never met him before and wasn't surprised when he had nothing persuasive to argue on Richard's behalf.

After ten minutes, the trial appeared to be over. Richard had committed unnamed crimes, had been seen doing them by people he had never heard of, and had been defended by a lawyer who offered not one word of convincing defense. Then Richard heard the judge say, "Wurmbrand, you have one minute. Do you wish to say anything?"

Richard stood. One minute wasn't long, but he used the time to talk about his faith. The judge interrupted him. "That's enough," he said, standing and leaving the room with the two lawyers. Two guards stepped forward and took Richard by the arms. Richard and Sabina locked eyes on each other before he was escorted from the room. Later that day Richard learned he had been sentenced to twenty-five years in prison. He would be seventy-four years old when he got out—unless the wheel of life and hope turned again.

By the end of the week, Richard had been beaten, shaved, and transported north to Gherla in Transylvania to begin his prison sentence. He had spent a little time incarcerated at Gherla Prison serving his previous jail term, and now he found conditions there still as brutal as he had experienced before. Ten thousand prisoners were crammed into a jail intended to house one-fifth that many. Prisoners slept two to a bunk or on the floor. The minimum punishment for any offense in the prison was twenty-five lashes. A doctor would stand nearby to make sure the prisoner did not die during the lashings, but many did. Each morning Richard looked out the small window of his crowded cell and saw piles of pine coffins outside filled with the bodies of prisoners who had died in the past twenty-four hours.

Richard did not escape his share of lashes, especially since he took every opportunity he could to preach. Sometimes he was housed in a cell filled with other pastors and priests in an attempt to keep the Christian leaders and their subversive ideas away from the other prisoners. Other times he found himself sharing cells with thieves and murderers. It made no difference to Richard what cell he was in. He tried to befriend his cellmates and lead them to know God.

Since the prisoners had nothing to do all day, they spent hours conversing and telling jokes. One day, in the course of one of these conversations, Richard was cheered up when he met a prisoner who knew someone he knew. He was sharing a cell with Ivan Grigore, a former Romanian soldier who had been responsible for murdering many Jews in Transnistria during the time Romania was allied with the Nazis. Richard told Ivan about his friend Borila, who had also been responsible for killing Jews in the same area during the war. He also told Ivan about the time

Sabina had gotten out of bed and embraced Borila as a Christian brother.

Ivan's eyes lit up when he learned this. "So that's what happened to Borila!" he exclaimed. "We couldn't understand it. I'd been with him in combat, but we were sent different ways in Bucharest. Then we met up again in Russia fighting alongside the Germans. None of us who knew Borila before could believe it. He was the first man to race out onto the battlefield to rescue someone under fire. He even saved the life of our commanding officer." Ivan shook his head. "Borila went from killing people for the fun of it to risking his life to save others."

"That's the power of God working in a man's soul," Richard replied.

The months turned into years. Richard was allowed no visitors, but a steady stream of news flowed into the jail from newly arrived prisoners. One new arrival in April 1961 reported that the Soviet Union had launched the first human into space. Four months later, at the end of August, another new arrival brought news that the Soviets had built a wall dividing Berlin, Germany, into two parts. In October 1962 the prisoners learned that the Soviet Union and the United States had been on the brink of war over the Soviets' attempt to install nuclear bombs on the island of Cuba, ninety miles from the United States. Although Richard listened to the news filtering in with new arrivals, he felt removed from much of it.

Life at Gherla Prison was monotonous, and any change in schedule or personnel was keenly noted.

One day electricians entered Richard's cell and installed four loudspeakers, one on each wall. Then they did the same in all the other cells. Everyone had an opinion on what this meant. The prisoners found out soon enough when the prison commandant began broadcasting "news" from Romania and around the world directly into the cells. The announcer told how millions of people had starved to death in the United States because greedy capitalists had pushed food prices so high only the rich could afford to eat. There were stories about prisoners who had been successfully reeducated and were now enjoying the "good life" in Romania with delicious food and lots of vodka and girlfriends. The broadcasts went on for hours each day. Some of them were entertaining, but most were depressing and reminded the prisoners of everything they were being deprived of.

Gradually the tone of the broadcasts began to change. The same phrases were repeated thousands of times in a row, and there was no way to escape hearing them. "Communism is good." "Christianity is stupid." "No one loves you." "Give up and make something of your life." "Where is your God now?"

Despite all the torture and mistreatment Richard had endured in prison, he decided that having to listen to this continuous barrage of words over the loudspeakers was one of the hardest things he'd had to endure. Still, he refused to renounce Christ and join the Communists.

In July 1963, Richard's stubbornness came to the attention of the prison commandant. "Perhaps it's time for you to come to the special block for treatment," he told Richard. "Few men ever return from there."

Later that day Richard was led from his cell, down a corridor, across the prison yard, and into another building. There he was placed in a white-tiled cell that reflected blinding white light from powerful concealed light bulbs. The heating, which functioned nowhere else in the prison, was turned to high in this cell, even though it was the middle of summer. Richard's handcuffs were left on so that all he could do was sit on the floor or lie on his back in the cell, where he sweated profusely. Loudspeakers continually blasted messages. "Nobody believes in Christ now. Nobody believes in Christ now. Nobody believes in Christ now. No one goes to church. No one goes to church. Give it up. Give it up. Give it up. Nobody believes in Christ now."

The messages blared all night long, the blinding light was left on, and the heat kept the cell at sauna-like temperatures.

After an uncomfortable night, Richard's handcuffs were removed, and he was taken to a new cell. This cell came with clean clothes, fresh sheets on the bed, even a table covered with a tablecloth, on top of which sat a vase holding a bouquet of flowers. Richard could scarcely fathom the change.

A little while later the prison commandant visited Richard in his new cell, pointing out to him that all the things surrounding him in the cell were a sample of the good life open to Richard if he renounced his faith and embraced Communism. The commandant also sent Richard a book to read titled *The Atheist's Guide.*

In the following weeks, Richard alternated between the beautiful cell with bed sheets, clean clothes, and fresh flowers and the cell with blinding white light, blaring loudspeakers, and stifling heat—and between the promise of what could be his if he denied his faith and what would continue to be his lot in life if he did not.

The "treatment" seemed to go on and on, but Richard would not do what his captors sought. He would not deny his faith. He would not embrace Communism.

After a time, General Negrea, deputy minister of the interior, visited Richard. The general offered him his freedom and a good salary. He would also make Richard the Lutheran bishop and guaranteed him a seat on the World Council of Churches if he would give up his "superstitious" message and adopt a Bible-friendly but "scientific" approach to the Christian faith. By now Richard had been back in prison for four and a half years. He was tired and sick. He hoped that Sabina was still waiting for him and that Mihai had found a way to survive, but he didn't know for sure. How tempting it was to think about seeing them again, about experiencing the outside world once more, about eating regular, nutritious meals and laughing with friends. After all the months of brainwashing, Richard struggled with what to do. Should he take the deal? Would anyone blame him for doing so?

In the end he thought about who his boss would be. Did he want God and his conscience to tell him what to do, or did he want the Romanian Securitate controlling his life? When he thought of it this way, he had no real choice. He would stay in prison knowing that one day he would either die there or be released.

Nearly a year later, on June 1, 1964, all the prisoners at Gherla were herded into a large hall. Something like this had never happened before. Major Alexandrescu, the prison commandant, strolled into the hall, flanked by his top guards. "The government has called for a general amnesty. You will all be freed soon," he announced.

Richard could barely believe what he was hearing. Was this another brainwashing trick? He would have to wait and see.

Amazingly, the prison did begin emptying out, a few hundred prisoners at a time. Richard waited for his turn to come. The population of Gherla Prison dwindled until only one hundred prisoners, Richard among them, were left. Then on June 21, 1964, Richard was taken from his cell and given a haircut and then clean clothes. Before he had time to take in all that was happening to him, the prison door opened and once again he was free. This time he had been locked up for five years and five months.

Outside the prison, Richard was put on a bus for the city of Cluj, twenty-five miles to the southwest. Through the bus windows everything sparkled in the sunlight, but Richard couldn't enjoy it. He was concerned about Sabina and Mihai. Were they still alive? Would they celebrate his release together?

When he reached Cluj, Richard made his way to the home of a Christian family he knew there. He borrowed their telephone and made a call, his fingers trembling as he dialed the number. He heard the sound of the phone ringing on the other end. Then someone picked it up. "Hello." It was Sabina's voice.

"It's me, Richard," he said.

There was a clattering sound on the line, and then silence.

Soon another voice, this time a man's voice, spoke on the other end.

"Father?"

"Yes," Richard said.

"Mother's fainted," Mihai told him. "We thought you were dead."

Chapter 15

"Let Me Show You My Credentials"

Once again Richard needed to be hospitalized following his release from prison. He weighed just ninety-eight pounds, and his feet and legs were swollen. Slowly, during the hospital stay, his health returned. And when the doctor released him, Richard returned to working with the underground church alongside Sabina and Mihai, who was now twenty-five years old.

Things with the underground church were much as they had been before Richard's second arrest. Small secret meetings continued to be held around Bucharest and out in the countryside, and spies were always in their midst.

After his release, Richard also began holding secret meetings with pastors in the state-sanctioned show churches. Some of these men told him how sorry they now were for cooperating with the government. Now they were stuck in their positions. If a show church pastor refused to inform on members of his congregation, he would be jailed and the church shuttered.

A few pastors Richard secretly contacted were so trusted by the government that they were allowed to leave the country to attend international Christian meetings, such as the annual meeting of the World Council of Churches. These pastors told Richard something he had suspected: people in the West had no idea what was really going on in Romania. Romania's Communist government produced Christian newspapers that circulated in other countries but were never seen in Romania. The government also forced the pastors as their representatives at the meetings to brag about the religious freedom they enjoyed in the country. If Romanian Christians were ever going to get help from the outside, someone needed to tell Western governments what was really going on.

Several of the pastors asked, "Who better to do that than Richard Wurmbrand?" They pointed out that Richard had been imprisoned by the government for his faith for fourteen years and that he had spoken to more men and women who had suffered for their faith than anyone else they knew.

For his part, Richard was content to stay in Romania and suffer alongside other Christians, but he could see the logic in reaching out to the West and convincing governments there to put pressure on Romania to change. Suffering Christians in all the Soviet Bloc countries needed a voice, and he could be that voice. But the real question was, would the Romanian government ever allow him to leave? And if so, where would he come up with the enormous sum of money that would be required to obtain a visa?

As Richard began thinking about this possibility, the Wurmbrands received a secret message from their friend Anutza Moise, who had fled Romania for Norway eighteen years before. In her message Anutza informed them that she had collected ten thousand dollars to ransom the family. The Romanian government, desperately in need of Western currency, had taken to selling Jewish citizens to Israel. The going rate was twenty-five hundred dollars per person, but the government wanted twice as much to let Richard leave for Israel.

The negotiations took many months. Sometimes the authorities told Richard he could go but his family wouldn't be allowed to join him. Other times he was told his official government file was stamped "Never to leave Romania." Still, Richard and Sabina persisted.

During this time, on March 22, 1965, following the death of Gheorghe Gheorghiu-Dej, Nicolae Ceauşescu became general secretary of the Romanian Communist Party and the country's new leader. Richard hoped this would lead to some positive changes in the country, but he doubted it would.

The months dragged on, and then one day Richard was called to police headquarters. He wasn't sure what to expect as he entered the building. To his surprise, an officer said the ransom money for Richard's release had been paid and his passport was ready.

"You can leave whenever you like and go wherever you like. And you can preach as often as you wish," the officer informed him. He then added, "Do not speak against us after you leave. Just preach your gospel. If you speak against us, you will be silenced—for good this time. We can hire a gangster to do it for us for one thousand dollars. Or we can bring you back here to Romania and silence you as we have done with other traitors. And remember, we can spread rumors about you that will destroy your reputation wherever you go. Do you understand?"

Richard nodded and walked out of police headquarters carrying his passport. Not only was he free to leave Romania, but also Sabina and Mihai could leave with him. As he made his way home, Richard thanked God for the turn of events.

On Wednesday, December 6, 1965, Richard, now fifty-six years old and accompanied by Sabina and Mihai, boarded an airplane in Bucharest bound for Rome, Italy. Two hundred people showed up to see them off. In Rome they would catch another plane to Israel, where the family planned to settle. It was hard for Richard to grasp that he was actually leaving his homeland. He was free. He would never be arrested for preaching again. He would no longer have to watch what he said regarding his faith for fear of spies. It seemed almost too good to be true.

When the plane landed in Ciampino Airport in Rome, Richard received a setback. The Israeli government had realized that the Wurmbrand family were Jews who believed in Jesus. As a result, it had revoked the family's visas to enter Israel. As disturbing as the news was, Richard was grateful that the Israeli authorities had not realized this earlier, or his family would probably never have gotten out of Romania.

With no visas for Israel, the family was stuck in political limbo, since they had no visas to enter and reside in another country. After two and a half nerve-wracking weeks to work it all out, the Wurmbrands were granted visas to visit Norway, where Anutza Moise and members of the Norwegian Israel Mission would welcome them.

Richard and Sabina hadn't seen Anutza since she fled Romania for Norway in March 1946. They thought they would never see her again on earth. When they stepped off the airplane in Oslo on December 23, they hugged Anutza and cried together and then hugged some more.

The following day, Christmas Eve, the Wurmbrands spent the evening with Anutza, singing hymns and carols and talking about old friends in Romania and new friends Anutza had made in the West. During the evening Richard looked out the window and saw before him a picture-perfect scene. Heavy snow lay on the ground and blanketed the trees.

Richard could see into several neighbors' houses. "Look Sabina! Come with me. I will show you something beautiful," he said, taking his wife by the hand and guiding her from window to window throughout Anutza's small house. "You can see other people's Christmas trees aglow with candles through their windows. There are no blinds or curtains. Nothing is shut up, because no one is afraid."

On Christmas Day Richard, Sabina, and Mihai attended the American Lutheran church in Oslo. Although the three of them did not understand Norwegian, they all spoke English, and the service was in English. Richard and Sabina wept through the meeting. It was so shocking to be in the midst of Christians who held Bibles in their hands and could sing loudly and listen to a sermon without fear.

When the service was over, Pastor Myrus Knutson asked Richard many questions, which he answered as honestly as he could. It seemed odd to him at first, though, not having to be cautious about the things he said in case a spy was eavesdropping.

After Christmas, the Norwegian Israel Mission arranged for Anutza Moise and the Wurmbrands to go to a convalescent home in the mountains for some rest. But within a few days of arriving there, crowds began gathering in the entranceway to see Richard, who had no idea he was that well known outside Romania.

After their rest in the mountains, the Wurmbrands headed back to Oslo, where Richard and Sabina spoke at many churches and events. Richard's message was always the same: All Christians are brothers and sisters, and God calls Christians in free countries to remember their brethren being persecuted and to reach out to help them in any way they can.

During this time Richard met people who said they had prayed for him and his family every single day for many years. He credited Anutza, along with the Norwegian and Swedish Lutheran churches, for rallying Scandinavian Christians of different denominations to pray for him and other persecuted Christians in Romania. Believers back home would be heartened to know that word of their plight had reached at least some of their brothers and sisters in the free world.

When Richard again attended a service at the American Lutheran church, Pastor Knutson came up to him and said, "I listened to everything you told me on Christmas Day, but I found it difficult to believe. We're told that Christians in Romania have religious freedom, when you clearly say they don't."

Richard nodded. It was hard for people to grasp just how much the Communists hated the gospel. Clearly, while some outsiders had discovered the truth, many other foreigners believed the Communists' false reports.

"So," the pastor continued, "I asked my friend at the U.S. Embassy to verify who you are. He got back to me today and declared that everything you say checks out. You are fully reliable."

Richard smiled. It felt good to be in a place where officials sought the truth instead of hiding behind lies.

Pastor Knutson arranged for Richard to speak in the chapel at the large NATO base on the edge of Oslo. At the meeting Richard spoke on the suffering and cost of being a Christian in a Communist country. At the end of the talk, a question-and-answer session was held. Colonel Sturdy, one of the base chaplains, asked Richard if he thought the West should or should not try to get along with Communists.

As soon as the question was asked, Richard stepped down from the podium, walked over, and pulled the wallet from the colonel's pocket. "Now let's get along," he said. The chapel fell silent. Then Richard added, "Of course we can't get along. I just stole from you. Communism has stolen over half of the world and taken people's freedom, their possessions, their health, their labor. Some people have cancer, but you don't hear of them coexisting with cancer. No, they resist it in any way they can. They cut it out of their bodies and take drugs to fight it. We need to fight the Communists too."

Colonel Sturdy stepped up to the podium. "Let's send this man to America with a message for those who think free nations should get along with Communist ones."

A collection plate was passed throughout the congregation. When they counted the money, they had raised enough for Richard and Sabina to go to the United States. Richard was stunned at the speed at which things were happening. He had been in Norway for only five weeks.

Soon plans were made. Richard and Sabina would go by ship across the Atlantic, while Mihai would go to Paris to stay with Sabina's older brother and his wife. Meanwhile, Colonel Sturdy helped set up a speaking itinerary on the East Coast of the United States for Richard and Sabina.

When Richard and Sabina arrived in New York City, Richard was stunned. The tall buildings, the mass of people, the cars and trucks, and the amazing array of food and other goods available for sale in stores was mind-boggling—unlike anything he had seen in Romania.

Richard began speaking about the persecuted church and the evils of Communism at the venues where Colonel Sturdy had arranged for him to speak. But as he and Sabina traveled from city to city, Richard began to find the meetings discouraging. Most were held in small military chapels, and it was obvious to him that many Americans had little interest in persecuted Christians. In the end, Richard decided that he and Sabina should return to Norway.

Before leaving, they went to Philadelphia to visit the only friend they knew in the United States, a Jewish Christian pastor. During the visit, Richard asked their friend to show him some of the sights of Philadelphia.

As the tour of Philadelphia progressed, the two men walked along a street and noticed that a large anti–Vietnam War rally was taking place inside an auditorium they were passing. Richard was amazed that such a rally could be freely held to protest the government's actions. The authorities in Romania would never allow such a thing. Curious, he headed into the building. A large crowd was gathered, and onstage a Presbyterian minister was addressing the people. As Richard listened to what the man was saying, he became outraged. The speaker was telling the crowd that Communist leaders, although atheists, were our friends and we should not oppose them.

Before he even realized it, Richard was walking to the front of the auditorium. He jumped up on stage and headed straight toward the microphone. As he did so, he shouted, "You know nothing of Communism. I'm a doctor in Communism. You should be on the side of Communism's victims, not defending such torturers."

"How can you be a doctor in Communism? Such a doctorate doesn't even exist," the Presbyterian minister snapped.

"Let me show you my credentials," Richard said, now standing in front of the crowd. With that he removed his shirt to reveal the scars and wounds that covered his torso from years of torture. "This is what the Communists did to me and the many others they tortured."

"And why would they do that?" the speaker asked.

"Because I am a clergyman like you. The Communists have tortured me and thousands of others like me simply because we are Christians. So why do you, a pastor, praise Communists and tell us that they are our friends, that we must not oppose them? You are a modern-day Judas!" Richard said into the microphone.

With that the crowd began booing the Presbyterian minister.

Moments later the police arrived and told Richard to put his shirt back on and then led him from the stage, though not before newspaper photographers had taken dramatic pictures of the incident.

The next day Richard was amazed to find a picture of himself shirtless on stage, his torture scars clearly visible, on the front page of the local newspaper. He learned that the picture had been printed in a number of other major newspapers as well. As a result, requests for interviews and invitations to speak at various venues began to pour in. Richard and Sabina had to postpone their return to Norway while they traveled the United States speaking and giving interviews.

The picture and news report on Richard that appeared in the newspapers caught the attention of Senator Thomas J. Dodd, vice chairman of the Senate Internal Security Subcommittee, in Washington, DC. Senator Dodd asked Richard to give his testimony before the subcommittee. Richard was honored but also mindful of what he had been told before leaving Romania—that he must not speak against the Romanian government, and if he did, he would face serious consequences. But as he thought about it, it became clear to him that he had come to the West to raise awareness of the plight of the persecuted church in Communist countries. What better place to do that than before a government committee of the most powerful nation in the West? Richard was amazed that such a committee existed to seek the truth rather than peddle lies, as happened in Romania. Yes, a risk was involved in testifying, but Richard was willing to take it.

On Friday morning, May 6, 1966, Richard, accompanied by Sabina, made his way to room 318 of the Old Senate Office in Washington, DC. Soon after he arrived, Senator Dodd called the subcommittee meeting to order, welcomed and introduced Richard, and then began questioning him. Richard answered the questions, giving as much detail as possible about the savage torture and persecution he and other prisoners had been subjected to in prison in Romania because of their faith.

As the questioning continued, Senator Dodd asked Richard if he was willing to show his scars to the members of the subcommittee. Once again Richard removed his shirt to reveal the wounds and scars inflicted on his body through torture. As he revealed his torture-ravaged torso, Richard said, "May it be very clear, it is not that I boast with these marks. I show to you the tortured body of my country, of my fatherland, and of my church, and they appeal to the American Christians and to all free men of America to think about our tortured body, and we do not ask you to help us. We ask you only one thing. Do not help our oppressors and do not praise them. You cannot be a Christian and praise the inquisitors of Christians. That is what I have to say."

Richard answered the questions asked by other subcommittee members for an hour and a half before the hearing was gaveled to a close.

Room 318 had been filled with reporters from American and international newspapers, along with the subcommittee members. The following day, reports of Richard's testimony before the Senate Internal Security Subcommittee appeared in newspapers around the world. Most of the reports were favorable. The article in the *New York Times* even carried a photo of Richard showing the committee members his scars.

Richard's testimony before the subcommittee was also published by the Senate as a booklet, which became an instant best seller. This was the kind of exposure of the treatment of Christians in Communist countries that Richard had hoped for when he left Romania.

Following his appearance before the subcommittee in Washington, DC, and the subsequent worldwide reporting on his testimony, Richard felt that the United States was the best place for him to be. It was where he could start an organization that would speak up for persecuted Christians in Communist countries, not just in Eastern Europe but also in China, Cuba, and North Korea. In November 1966, Richard, Sabina, and Mihai immigrated to the United States.

Chapter 16

Voice of the Martyrs

In early 1967, Richard sat in the living room of his duplex dictating the story of his treatment by Communists onto a reel-to-reel tape recorder. Sabina sat by his side. Together they wept as they relived the nightmare of persecution and torture they had endured over the previous twenty-three years. By now Richard and Sabina, along with Mihai and his new wife, Judith, were living in Southern California.

Judith had her own story to tell. She had been raised in a traditional Jewish home in Bucharest, where she met Mihai and the Wurmbrands several times before emigrating from Romania with her family to Israel in 1961 at the age of sixteen. In Israel she had a chance meeting with the Levys. Isaac Levy was one of the thugs who had harassed Richard and his congregation after Richard spoke out at the Congress of the Cults in 1945. Isaac became a Christian and later married Anika King's mother after her husband, the hypnotist-doctor, died.

The Levys were strong members of the underground church before moving to Israel. The couple befriended Judith in Israel and shared the gospel with her. Judith became a Christian and set out for missionary school in Germany. She wrote to Mihai occasionally, and he invited her to visit him in Paris, where the two fell in love. In California on December 20, 1966, Mihai Wurmbrand and Judith Tesler were married.

The extended Wurmbrand family had one mission: to tell the world what was happening behind the curtain of Communism and bring aid to those who suffered there. To help accomplish this, they set up an organization, which they named Jesus to the Communist World. They used their first one-hundred-dollar donation to start a monthly newsletter. Five hundred copies of the first edition were printed and sent out to anyone they had met along the way and to friends of friends. "Read and Pass It On" was printed in large letters on the front of every copy. Richard hoped the newsletter would be another step in reaching the world on behalf of those Christians who had no voice.

The story Richard dictated onto the reel-to-reel tape recorder was turned into a book titled *Tortured for Christ*, which also became an instant best seller. Through the newsletter and the book, the eyes of many were opened to what was happening to Christians in Communist lands.

Soon churches began to inquire about how they could help. Richard and Sabina began traveling extensively, telling Christians in churches and at rallies what they could do to help. Richard also challenged idealistic young Communists in free countries to think about what life would be like under a Communist regime. He told anyone who would listen, "Don't think you have only a few Communists in your country. That's what we thought in Romania, and look what happened to us. The free world is full of small, dedicated Communist groups waiting for their day to seize power. They will never give up. Communism is like a tiger. You can play with a small tiger, but do not be fooled. When it grows up, it will eat you."

Following the success of *Tortured for Christ*, Richard wrote another book, *In God's Underground*, giving more details of his life under Communism. Around the world, Christian youth groups, Sunday schools, and women's groups began raising money to support the ministry of Jesus to the Communist World. With this money, the organization bought printing presses and published Gospel booklets in many languages. They printed thousands of copies of the Gospels in Korean to be attached to balloons that would be released on the border between South and North Korea. The wind would carry the Gospel-laden balloons far into North Korea. Before long a quarter of a million Scripture portions had been sent to North Korea in this way.

Meanwhile, Bibles were smuggled into Communist countries in false-bottom suitcases or were dropped from airplanes. Some were sealed in plastic bags and dropped overboard from boats in international waters, where the current would take them and wash them up on the shores of China, Siberia, and Cuba. Radio stations around the world began beaming the message of hope in fifty languages, and large portions of the Bible were read at dictation speed over the airwaves so that anyone listening could write down the words.

During this time the extended Wurmbrand family was changing and growing too. In 1970 Mihai, who now went by the Americanized name Michael, became an ordained Lutheran pastor. Then on June 12, 1972, Judith gave birth to a daughter, whom they named Amely.

Richard and Sabina divided their time between working with Jesus to the Communist World in the United States, writing books, and preaching around the world. When he spoke, Richard drew large crowds, which sometimes were hostile to his message. In Basel, Switzerland, Richard was preaching to a packed auditorium of four thousand people when Communist Party youth stormed the place, chanting and raising their fists in the Communist salute. Police had to use tear gas to break up the protest. Although the Romanian authorities had not, as far as Richard knew, tried to have him killed or kidnapped and returned to the country, during 1972 Romania's Communist government declared publicly that "the duty of the church is to fight against Wurmbrand."

As the years went by, Richard expanded the focus of his ministry to include Communist guerrillas who were terrorizing Christians in much of Central and South America. Then, to encompass those Christians who were being persecuted and killed by Muslim extremists in Somalia, Ethiopia, South Yemen, Iraq, Angola, and Mozambique, the ministry's name was changed from Jesus to the Communist World to Voice of the Martyrs (VOM).

In 1977 Richard turned sixty-eight, an age at which many men thought of retiring. But not Richard, who felt he was just getting going. In October that year, Judith gave birth to a son, Alex.

Richard was spurred on in his ministry through the 1970s and 1980s by the growth of Communism and persecution around the world. In 1975, Communist North Vietnam overran South Vietnam to form a united Communist country. The same year, the Communist Khmer Rouge took control of Cambodia, Vietnam's neighbor. Their rule of Cambodia was brutal. They isolated the country from all foreign influences. Schools, hospitals, and factories were closed, banking was abolished, all religions were outlawed, private property was confiscated, and the people were relocated from urban areas to collective farms in the countryside to work as forced laborers. Over a million and a half people either were executed by the Khmer Rouge or died of starvation. In the West, Cambodia became known as the Killing Fields.

Then in 1979 the Soviet Union invaded Afghanistan. At the same time, children in the Soviet Union were being placed in psychiatric asylums for refusing to deny Christ. In Eastern Bloc countries, including

Romania, economies had stagnated. Everything there seemed to be in short supply as people tried desperately to make ends meet. It wasn't just the Communists who were persecuting Christians. In Islamic Iran Christians were being imprisoned and hanged for their faith.

All of this kept Richard and Voice of the Martyrs busy doing all the ministry they could to reach out in practical ways and telling Westerners about the plight of their Christian brothers and sisters in other countries. As Cambodian Christians sought to flee the Communist onslaught in their country, VOM supplied rice to keep them from starving. In Mozambique VOM provided canoes, food, and clothing so that starving Christians could travel and share the gospel with their Communist enemies. VOM also began underground printing presses in a number of Communist countries, six of them in China, where they printed hymnals, copies of the Gospels, and Christian books.

On March 24, 1989, Richard celebrated his eightieth birthday. Several weeks later, in April, a student-led demonstration began in Tiananmen Square in Beijing, China. The students called for democracy, greater accountability from China's leaders, freedom of the press, and freedom of speech. For a month and a half, the protest went on, with up to a million people gathering in the square to demonstrate. Then on June 4, 1989, the Chinese government moved to repress the protest, sending in troops armed with assault rifles and tanks to disperse the crowd. By the time the demonstration was suppressed, an estimated one thousand protesters had been massacred in Tiananmen Square. Once again Richard watched as the iron fist of Communism quashed those who disagreed with its ideology. He could only imagine the reprisals that would follow. How many young Chinese men and women would be thrown into prison to be tortured and persecuted for their beliefs as the Communists had done to him in Romania?

While China's Communist government was cracking down on its citizens, something different was beginning to happen in the Eastern Bloc countries. It was something Richard for years had been praying would happen.

In March 1985 Mikhail Gorbachev had become leader of the Soviet Union. He took over a country whose economy was a mess. Economic and political reforms were desperately needed, and Gorbachev introduced these reforms in the form of *glasnost* and *perestroika.* He was hoping that the reforms would help the Soviet Union become more prosperous and productive.

Glasnost was intended to make the country more open politically. The remaining vestiges of Stalinist repression, such as book banning and the ever-present secret police, were swept aside. Political prisoners were released, newspapers were permitted to print criticism of the government, and political parties besides the Communist Party were permitted to participate in elections.

Perestroika was supposed to revive the Soviet economy. Gorbachev believed that private initiative would lead to economic innovation. As a result, individuals and cooperatives were allowed to own businesses, and workers were given the right to strike for better wages and conditions.

Gorbachev also announced that Soviet troops would be withdrawn from Afghanistan and that he would reduce the Soviet military presence in Eastern Bloc countries. This, coupled with the glasnost reforms, had a huge impact, sparking peaceful revolutions in Eastern Bloc countries. In 1989 noncommunist trade unionists from the Solidarity movement in Poland bargained with the Communist government for the free election of the president and 35 percent of the members of Parliament. In Hungary the government allowed free association and assembly and opened the country's borders with the West.

On November 9, 1989, Richard, like so many others in the West, watched his television in wonderment as the Berlin Wall, the most visible symbol of the Communist division of Europe, was torn down and East Germans swarmed to the West. Later that month Czechoslovakia's Communist government was overthrown.

A new wind of freedom was sweeping across Eastern Europe. It soon blew into Romania, where thousands of people began protesting the oppressive Communist regime. Nicolae Ceauşescu ordered the protest repressed, and the army and police fired into the crowd of protestors, killing dozens of people. But the protestors persisted, and the soldiers soon came over to their side. In the face of the ongoing protest, Ceauşescu was forced to flee Bucharest but was arrested by the army in the countryside. An interim government was set up and a trial quickly held. On December 25, 1989, Nicolae Ceauşescu and his wife were executed. It was almost too much for Richard to comprehend. His homeland at last was throwing off the shackles of forty-five years of Communist rule.

Romania's borders were opened, and within a few days, Voice of the Martyrs workers sent semitrucks filled with aid across the border. In Bucharest workers set up a Christian bookstore, which they named Stephanus Bookstore and stocked it with books and Bibles. Three months later it had sold 20,000 books and 300,000 Bibles.

On May 14, 1990, the airplane carrying eighty-one-year-old Richard Wurmbrand and seventy-seven-year-old Sabina Wurmbrand touched down at Otopeni Airport in Bucharest. The couple had been away from their homeland for twenty-five years. A large crowd of old friends and new faces had gathered to meet them as they deplaned. It was wonderful for them all to be able to embrace one another openly in public and sing hymns together in the airport terminal.

Although overwhelmed by the welcome, Richard couldn't help but think of all the people not there to greet him, those who had been killed by the Nazis and the Communists. As they were driven into the city, Richard noted that even the architecture had changed in the time he had been away. Nicolae Ceauşescu had leveled a great swath of Bucharest in order to build enormous government buildings and housing blocks modeled after the concrete monstrosities built in Pyongyang, North Korea. The Jewish people were gone too. Many were dead, while others had immigrated to Israel. When Richard left Romania, about 150,000 Jews were living in the country. Now only 9,000 remained.

In Bucharest Richard was widely received, preaching in many churches and even on public television. When he spoke, his message was always the same. Although it was understandable to hate Communism and all it had done to Romania, Christians must never hate the Communist person. God calls Christians to reach out to all people in love, to turn the other cheek to those who have persecuted them. Richard told his audiences how he and Sabina had helped Nazi workers get back to Germany after the Soviets entered Romania in 1944. He asked others to extend that same compassion to Communists now so that the true power of the gospel could be clearly seen at work.

Richard felt most at home in the VOM bookstore, where many people came to see him. Soon after Richard arrived in Romania, the bookstore manager took him to an area the government allowed them to use for book storage. It was located in a lower basement beneath what was being called Ceauşescu's Palace, the massive new building in the heart of the city built to house Romania's government. Among the hundreds of structures that had been demolished to make way for the new building was Uranus Prison. As Richard descended the steps to the basement, he realized that the prison dungeon was still intact and he was being led to the cell in which he had been kept in solitary confinement for nearly three years. He was astonished to find stacks of his books in the cell. Richard knew it was more than a coincidence. It was God's way of telling him that He had been at work all along, that Richard's faith and patience had paid off. The wheel of life and hope had turned, not just a little, but completely. Richard thought of his torturers over the years who had told him Communism would last forever. Then he called to mind Isaiah 40, verse 8: "The grass withers, the flower fades, but the word of our God will stand forever."

Following their trip to Romania, Richard and Sabina returned to the United States. From there Richard watched as change continued to sweep across the Communist countries of Eastern Europe. On April 29, 1991, the old Communist People's Republic of Albania was dissolved and the democratic Republic of Albania founded. Then, on December 25, 1991, exactly two years after Romanian Communist leader Nicolae Ceauşescu and his wife were executed, Mikhail Gorbachev resigned as president of the Soviet Union. The following day the Soviet Union officially broke up and ceased to exist.

In the wake of this change, Voice of the Martyrs moved in, opening a Christian bookstore in Moscow and distributing over one million illustrated New Testaments to children in Albania, Romania, Moldavia, Russia, Ukraine, and Bulgaria. The organization also kept its focus on other suffering and persecuted

Christians. In the United States, Christians donated thousands of used Bibles and Christian books that were sent to Nigeria, where hundreds of churches had been destroyed by Muslims.

In March 1995 Richard turned eighty-six. By now both he and Sabina were experiencing significant health problems. Richard needed to spend more time in bed as old injuries from his mistreatment and torture in prison caused his spine to deteriorate. Sabina was diagnosed with stomach cancer. She underwent surgery for the cancer and slowly regained her strength. Despite their health issues, Richard and Sabina returned to Romania for the official opening of VOM's Agape Children's Home, where orphans and street children could be cared for in a loving Christian environment.

Back home in Southern California, Sabina looked after Richard as his health continued to deteriorate. However, in 2000 she suffered a relapse of her stomach cancer and died on August 11 that year at age eighty-seven. Richard was too ill to attend her funeral, but fifteen hundred other people gathered to bid farewell to the woman who had stood staunchly at his side for sixty-four years.

Six months later, on February 17, 2001, Richard died peacefully. Fifty years had passed since he was taken to the Death Room at Tirgul-Ocna Prison, where he was expected to be dead within days. Richard was buried beside Sabina at Rose Hills Cemetery in Whittier, California. Engraved on his tombstone are the words from Luke's Gospel "Why Seek Ye the Living Among the Dead?"

Around the world, memorial services were held for Richard, and his obituary appeared in many national newspapers. More important, his words continued to be carried across the world in the twenty books he wrote during his lifetime. At the time of his death, millions of copies of them were in print, and they had been translated into seventy-five languages.

In 2006 Romanian television conducted a vote to discover who Romanians considered to be the one hundred greatest Romanians of all time. When the votes were tallied, Richard Wurmbrand was number five on the list. The life of the man who had served Christ unswervingly and suffered greatly for his faith had indeed deeply impacted his fellow countrymen.

Bibliography

Cole, Jack. *Richard and Sabina: A Biography of the Rev. Richard Wurmbrand and His Wife Sabina.* N.p.: Xlibris, 2000.

Drewery, Mary. *Richard Wurmbrand: The Man Who Came Back.* London: Hodder and Stoughton, 1974.

Mackenzie, Catherine. *Richard Wurmbrand: A Voice in the Dark.* Fearn, UK: Christian Focus, 1997.

Moise, Anutza. *A Ransom for Wurmbrand.* Grand Rapids: Zondervan, 1972.

Wurmbrand, Judy. *Escape from the Grip.* London: Hodder and Stoughton, 1979.

Wurmbrand, Mihai. *Between Hammer and Sickle.* Glendale, CA: Diane, 1972.

Wurmbrand, Richard. *From Suffering to Triumph!* Grand Rapids: Kregel, 1991.

———. *In God's Underground.* New York: Fawcett, 1968.

———. *Tortured for Christ.* Bartlesville, OK: Living Sacrifice, 1998.

———. *With Christ on the Jewish Road.* Bartlesville, OK: Living Sacrifice, 1970.

Wurmbrand, Sabina. *The Pastor's Wife.* New York: John Day, 1971.